HOW TO SHAKE THE UNSHAKABLE *by the* TRUE ANOINTING

THE TRUE MANNA

THE GLORY OF GOD

Order this book online at www.trafford.com
or email orders@trafford.com

Most Trafford titles are also available at major online book retailers.

Scripture quotations marked KJV are from the Holy Bible, King James Version (Authorized Version). First published in 1611. Quoted from the KJV Classic Reference Bible, Copyright © 1983 by The Zondervan Corporation.

Print information available on the last page.

ISBN: 978-1-4907-6188-6 (sc)
ISBN: 978-1-4907-6189-3 (e)

Trafford rev. 06/30/2015

www.trafford.com
North America & international
toll-free: 1 888 232 4444 (USA & Canada)
fax: 812 355 4082

Not by might, nor by power, but by my spirit, saith the Lord of hosts.

CONTENTS

CONTENTS

PREFACE

I read this book and I want to address to all the readers.

This book is not only a book like other, it contains wisdom and deliverance power to set lives free.

Dr. Raha Mugisho teaches on different biblical principal that can change your life.

Some of the quotes I loved while reading are:

-Nothing is important than God, so He must be the priority of our entire concept of life. Nobody shall take his place in our heart, in our mind and in our spirit.

-Second quote I liked in this book. Better have the daily discipline to worship God first and move on later. God created us for the sole order to have a holy faith and in communion with him.

The primary responsibility of par Insult, selfish, but praying culture, dedication, giving and tithing, love, holiness, humility). The first responsibility of a Pastor is a new convert to a true devotee. That who ignores discipline despises himself. Prov. 15: 32

By this quote alone, this book is teaching the readers the need to respect the word of God. So many home and churches are destroyed because of rebellious children. Also the book is showing the blessing behind Love, giving, praying tithing, etc.

-Third and last, I believe that his book by itself is a miracle you need. You can easily find powerful biblical verses and scriptural declaration of faith that shakes the unshakable by the anointing of the Holy Spirit. The purpose of the Holy Spirit is to take the kingdom of God all over the earth. This book teaches you how to trust the power of God, the faith in the Lord Jesus Christ and the Moving by the Holy Spirit.

Last declaration I loved while reading is the relationship of the author with the Holy Spirit.

God bless you as you read this book let it be the voice of God that guides and speaks the life of God through your Life. In the name of Jesus Christ. Amen.

Shalom
Pastor Silver Amissi Matanda

DEDICATION

This book is dedicated to Bishops, J.B. Masinde, Arthur Kitonga, J.M. LUGERERO, Leon Sangara, Kikunda Jeremie and Mugisho Charles.

Thank you for being always in the field of God.

Servant of God, Brother RAHA MUGISHO

FOUNDER OF RHEMA PENTECOSTAL CHURCHES/SEI

PRESIDENT OF CHRISTIAN INTERNATIONAL SOLIDARITY

Godfaithful777@yahoo.com

ACKNOWLEDGEMENTS

I want to acknowledge Bishops, Elisha Muliri, Bondo Daudi, Amisi Uwezo, my dear brothers and sisters, cousins and nephews, and spiritual sons, Mr. Lamuel Byamugisha, Basirwa Chifizi, Pedro and Mapendo Ntambuka, Dr. Mugisho Muhaya. I know how, both day and night, you were always my consolation and help.

May God bless you richly. THERE IS TIME TO EACH THING IN THIS WORLD. ONLY TRUE LOVE CAN BE A GOOD MEDICINE FOR ALL OF US. I LOVE YOU, TOO. THE KING DAVID'S WISDOM

THE GLORY OF THIS PRESENT HOUSE WILL BE GREATER THAN THE GLORY OF THE FORMER HOUSE, SAYS THE LORD ALMIGHTY. AND IN THIS PLACE I WILL GRANT PEACE, DECLARES THE LORD ALMIGHTY (Haggai 2:9).

INTRODUCTION

In these revelations I want to emphasize the meaning of these capital realities.

1. Nothing is more important than God, so He must be the priority of our entire concept of life. Nobody shall take his place in our hearts, in our minds and in our spirits. It means that all imagination of things is nothing compared to the most high who must fill our hearts, our spirits and our dreams. If we do not understand this principle we shall have somewhere and somehow an idol which will affect our good relationship with God. Worship God first and then serve Him and He shall give you the desire of your heart.

2. God is able and willing to perform his plan in our lives when we surrender to him completely. Remove from your mind the competitors of God in all your activities. Let's give to God our time and consider the importance of it. Do not expose your time for nonsensical activities. Your time is very precious and it is the first precious offering we have to give to God. Give God enough time in your life. This is needed and God wants you and your time. You have to give God your best every single day of your life because tomorrow could be too late.

3. Keep believing God in all things and do not give up. Though your imagination be wrong, your experience be wrong, the words of people be wrong, but the Word of God true (Romans 3:4).

4. The sin of Satan was not adultery or another worse thing that people are imagining but it was the rebellion against God. And the huge work in which he succeeded has caused the majority of all human beings to experience the impact of rebellion. Humans revolt against God from the morning to the night. They easily yield to the suggestions of the devil rather than God. Satan is the enemy number one of the human being but humans are imitating his sin in many of our decisions. It is impossible for God to make his habitation inside people because of this revolt. Why are Christians quarrelling, mistreating

others, living in selfishness, false accusation, gossip, strong worldly desire and competition, lack of compassion and the list goes on...? That is the act of rebellion against God and such behavior resembles the devil. The decision is yours; the choice is yours. God is still looking for obedient and holy instruments. Satan is the fiercest enemy of humanity. He is already condemned and all he does is to bring the great numbers of people to share that curse brought on through rebellion. The first thing we must confess and win is the sin of rebellion. A house divided against itself cannot stand and this is the weapon the devil is using to divide servants of God and believers, thus bringing dissension. Wake up, children of God, and be united in Jesus.

5. Better to have the daily discipline to WORSHIP GOD first and go to other things later. God created us for the unique purpose of enjoying a holy and faithful fellowship with Him. The first responsibility of parents is to educate their children to fear God and to avoid the sin of rebellion against God (no insults or selfishness but a culture of prayer, dedication, giving and tithing, love, holiness, humility). The first responsibility of a pastor is to make a new convert a true worshipper. He who ignores discipline despises himself (Prov. 15: 32).

CHAPTER ONE

FIVE POWERFUL FINGERS OF REVIVAL AND SEVEN OBSTACLES OF COMPLETE FREEDOM

TO ROOT OUT, AND TO PULL DOWN, AND TO DESTROY, AND TO THROW DOWN, TO BUILD, AND TO PLANT MEANS WE MASTER THESE PRINCIPLES.

1. LOVE
2. FAITH
3. HOLINESS
4. TRUE WORSHIP
5. FRESH ANOINTING

These five powerful fingers have strong bed-sheets of love escorted by faith, dwelling in holiness, supported by adoration, signed by the anointing.

I
LOVE

1. Love isn't an option but an order; we have to love one another. There is no alternative; there are no more words. Love has to be our native language and the bond between the children of God. No discrimination, no racism, no tribalism in the family of God. If I have the power to help somebody and I refuse to secure him, it is a failure in the love of God. It is possible to read love in our eyes, to feel love in our voices and in our words. Love is equal to itself; you cannot replace it

with another thing. Love exhibits generosity everywhere. It is unique in the road of action because it provokes joy everywhere and demonstrates salvation. The presence of God is manifested in his activation of life for many afflicted people. In fact it is stronger than death and people chase after its power. Love never fails; it is a rare product for which the world has a strong need. If the whole world could accept it, nowhere would people go to war or fight each other because inside them there is forgiveness, tolerance, understanding and they don't repay evil for evil. There is no pride, arrogance, or jealousy in them. Gossip and false accusations do not have room in them. God is love and He always exposes love everywhere so his children may qualify and walk in excellence.

2. This love always has an open room for good. We cannot be limited because of pain and offense, because the love drives us to right reactions according the fruit of the Spirit. Not that are we exhibiting good reactions but right, discerning what is the will of God in all we are doing. True love always escorts these fruits of the Spirit: Joy, Peace, Patience, Kindness, Goodness and Self Control. There is no way that we should authorize the flesh to direct us but the Spirit. It is certain that love bears inside us a door of forgiveness, compassion, mercy and another way of reparation. We have not only to exhibit positive reactions but right reactions, which cannot disturb the freedom of innocence. For example, if I hide a thief in my house and I expose others to insecurity by his behavior, I am not doing right. The right action should be to look for a way to correct him. I may forgive him but not endorse him in my relationship. That is ignorance, not love. Anybody with wrong faith can easily destroy other people who are exposed to him; better to be separated from him in peace. This separation in peace with this thief and the man with wrong faith is a right reaction. The love of God doesn't mean that we will bring a serpent and live with it; surely it will harm us. What we can to the wrongdoer is to give him an opportunity to change. And the special issue for him to consider is the gospel of Jesus. We cannot give a false testimony to save a fake person; not at all, we have to say the truth in all circumstances. Loving a lie is not right but a sin. A right reaction in the Spirit is a good thing but a good reaction according to tradition and even routine may be not right if it is not obedient to the Word of God.

3. **Love in Action, Roman 12**

    [9] Love must be sincere. Hate what is evil; cling to what is good. [10] Be devoted to one another in love. Honor one another above yourselves. [11] Never be lacking in zeal, but keep your spiritual fervor, serving the Lord. [12] Be joyful in hope, patient in affliction, faithful in prayer. [13] Share with the Lord's people who are in need. Practice hospitality.

¹⁴ Bless those who persecute you; bless and do not curse. ¹⁵ Rejoice with those who rejoice; mourn with those who mourn. ¹⁶ Live in harmony with one another. Do not be proud, but be willing to associate with people of low position. [c] Do not be conceited.

¹⁷ Do not repay anyone evil for evil. Be careful to do what is right in the eyes of everyone.¹⁸ If it is possible, as far as it depends on you, live at peace with everyone. ¹⁹ Do not take revenge, my dear friends, but leave room for God's wrath, for it is written: "It is mine to avenge; I will repay,"[d] says the Lord. ²⁰ On the contrary:

"If your enemy is hungry, feed him;

if he is thirsty, give him something to drink.

In doing this, you will heap burning coals on his head."[e]

²¹ Do not be overcome by evil, but overcome evil with good.

ROMANS 13

Love Fulfills the Law

⁸ Let no debt remain outstanding, except the continuing debt to love one another, for whoever loves others has fulfilled the law. ⁹ The commandments, "You shall not commit adultery," "You shall not murder," "You shall not steal," "You shall not covet,"[a] and whatever other command there may be, are summed up in this one command: "Love your neighbor as yourself."[b] ¹⁰ Love does no harm to a neighbor. Therefore love is the fulfillment of the law

Matthew 12: 25

²⁵ Jesus knew their thoughts and said to them, "Every kingdom divided against itself will be ruined, and every city or household divided against itself will not stand.

How can we pray together when we are separated? How can we expect a revival when we close its door? How can God speak with us when we become his enemy and we refuse to serve him? The church must work heartily on it and come to repent of this sin of hatred and condemnation; we must love one another and support each other so we may reap a true revival. We cannot stand being divided while we pretend to dwell in one body.

Matthew 5

⁴⁰ And if anyone wants to sue you and take your shirt, hand over your coat as well. ⁴¹ If anyone forces you to go one mile, go with them two miles. ⁴² Give to the one who asks you, and do not turn away from the one who wants to borrow from you.

4. LOVE IS LIFE AND NOT A STRANGE STORY

Love is not in words but in actions
Love is not what you see but it speaks out loud
Love is not only what you think but what you do
Love is not a dream; it is the reality
Love is not a mystery but visible reactions
Love must be shared and not held selfishly
Love looks for the benefit of another human being
Love brings joy amidst sorrows
Love is needed everywhere
Love is the solution forever
Love is an excellent shelter
Love is a living light in the heart, spirit and soul
Love is incomparable; you need it now
Love is a remedy without medicine
Love is not the desire of the flesh
Love is the heart speaking sincerity
Love is not lust but a precious present
Love doesn't carry death but produces life
Love is the fundamental answer of inner need
Love fills the cup of satisfaction
Love is the container of good surprises.
Love doesn't look for mistakes but for reparation
Love never counts the number of mess ups
Love is new every day and forgets the past
Love has no a date of expiration
Love brings hope even in the desert.
Love itself is life and hope
Love always gives another opportunity
Faith can never replace love
Hope can never replace love
Corruption can never replace love
God is love
I LOVE YOU
1 Corinthians 13
King James Version (KJV)

13 Though I speak with the tongues of men and of angels, and have not charity, I am become as sounding brass, or a tinkling cymbal.

² And though I have the gift of prophecy, and understand all mysteries, and all knowledge; and though I have all faith, so that I could remove mountains, and have not charity, I am nothing.

13. And now abideth faith, hope, charity, these three; but the greatest of these is charity.

5. The actual church fails regarding the kind of love that Christ wants in his body. The Church has to correct the way she is behaving concerning the sharing of blessing and hospitality. It is the responsibility of churches to support the ministers but the spiritual leaders have also the duty to care about poor members and the needy in the church. With millions of dollars in the possession of a leader, why doesn't he create jobs for believers? And he can continue to receive tithes so nobody shall suffer. Better to think of others and to always be a blessing.

Acts 4: ³² And the multitude of them that believed were of one heart and of one soul: neither said any of them that ought of the things which he possessed was his own; but they had all things common.

³³ And with great power gave the apostles witness of the resurrection of the Lord Jesus: and great grace was upon them all.

³⁴ Neither was there any among them that lacked: for as many as were possessors of lands or houses sold them, and brought the prices of the things that were sold,

³⁵ And laid them down at the apostles' feet: and distribution was made unto every man according as he had need.

³⁶ And Joses, who by the apostles was surnamed Barnabas, (which is, being interpreted, the son of consolation,) a Levite, and of the country of Cyprus,

³⁷ Having land, sold it, and brought the money, and laid it at the apostles' feet.

Example of generosity: 2 Cor 8: 3-5 for to their power, I bear record, yea, and beyond their power they were willing of themselves;

⁴ Praying us with much intreaty that we would receive the gift, and take upon us the fellowship of the ministering to the saints.

⁵ And this they did, not as we hoped, but first gave their own selves to the Lord, and unto us by the will of God.

Things are changing in the worst way because of lack of love. But it is not too late. We have the time to correct our faults and be a blessing for the work of God, and to the believers throughout the entire world if possible.

We have to push others materially and financially, so they can be efficient in the gospel and travel to every corner to share the spiritual gift to many. Better to have the spirit of receiving other preachers with different subjects of messages according the Holy Spirit. Why limit God by staying only with the preferred message? The Holy Spirit knows the real need of the church. Do not make the church of God your own business. It is not yours; it is for God. The leaders have to take time to discern what is the will of God for every visitor who comes to the Church. If not he shall close the door to an angel who should bring the remedy of the army of the Lord. Other ministers only invite particular preachers who will raise enough money that they will share after the service. This becomes a mockery to God. If you have a message of repentance or of holiness, few will give you the altar. However the church needs this kind of sermon.

The people of God do not have to imitate the style of Egypt. They have to present holy strategy, holy style and holy language. Even in their dances, self control is necessary. If the way to dress becomes seductive, it becomes a sin.

Number 23

[9] Far from the top of the rocks I see him, and from the hills I behold him: lo, the people shall dwell alone, and shall not be reckoned among the nations.

[10] Who can count the dust of Jacob, and the number of the fourth part of Israel? Let me die the death of the righteous, and let my last end be like his!

Believers fail to reflect this love because they learned to focus all their attention on a category of men (prophets and miracle preachers) and not the entire body of Christ. Thus, most of them become hypocrites. God wants them to repent, embracing the true love. Not everybody should have the same gifts; we work together in the body of Christ, completing each other.

Fanatism and tribalism with discrimination has entered the Church. Few are looking for the benefit of Christ but for their own. Some are 'for Paul' and other are 'for Peter' instead of being united in the body of Christ.

1 Cor 3: [4] For while one saith, I am of Paul; and another, I am of Apollos; are ye not carnal?

[5] Who then is Paul, and who is Apollos, but ministers by whom ye believed, even as the Lord gave to every man?

[6] I have planted, Apollos watered; but God gave the increase.

[7] So then neither is he that planteth any thing, neither he that watereth; but God that giveth the increase.

[8] Now he that planteth and he that watereth are one: and every man shall receive his own reward according to his own labour.

[9] For we are labourers together with God: ye are God's husbandry, ye are God's building.

[21] Therefore let no man glory in men. For all things are yours;

[22] Whether Paul, or Apollos, or Cephas, or the world, or life, or death, or things present, or things to come; all are yours;

[23] And ye are Christ's; and Christ is God's.

The church of Christ is one and indivisible.

Love must be the first and great character visible to each person. A believer cannot suffer for any need when we have the capacity to mobilize our resources to meet his needs. This is also the duty of the church to help each other. That's what it means to love each other.

The church of this time has a high motivation to form a religious domain and not the body of Christ. It is so sad to see how most of the Christian leaders have the ambition to build their kingdom where another messenger of Christ cannot have access in order to attack the apostasy.

It is also very dangerous the way the Word is oriented to exploit believers, pushing them not for repentance but to give only money excessively. I know that the distorted ministers will not like this advice but they have to know that they are accountable to God for all the false teaching they are doing to enrich themselves and to exalt their names and not the name of our Savior Jesus- Christ. Let the church give heartily and not by force or lies from the Word concerning the blessings. God blesses those who give cheerfully and not in fleshly competition.

The owner of the Church is outside knocking at the door while the religious leader is refusing to open.

I give you a warning as the apostle of Christ to repent and give the true Word to the sheep. Where will you go with all the rubbish of this world when your spirit shall depart from your body?

Take the good example of T.L. OSBORN who evangelized the whole world and in his time, most of the preachers got the loudspeaker to preach the gospel. His books were much anointed and pushed us to go everywhere to preach the gospel. May God supply other ministers with the heart of T.L. OSBORN to bring true revival in this world. T.L Osborn supported thousands of African preachers and they did excellent jobs—both those in America and the world.

Rev: 3 [19] As many as I love, I rebuke and chasten: be zealous therefore, and repent.

²⁰ Behold, I stand at the door, and knock: if any man hear my voice, and open the door, I will come in to him, and will sup with him, and he with me.

²¹ To him that overcometh will I grant to sit with me in my throne, even as I also overcame, and am set down with my Father in his throne.

²² He that hath an ear, let him hear what the Spirit saith unto the churches.

II
FAITH

HEBREWS 11

1 Now faith is the substance of things hoped for, the evidence of things not seen.

⁶ But without faith it is impossible to please him: for he that cometh to God must believe that he is, and that he is a rewarder of them that diligently seek him.

HEBREWS 10

³⁵ Cast not away therefore your confidence, which hath great recompence of reward.

³⁶ For ye have need of patience, that, after ye have done the will of God, ye might receive the promise.

³⁷ For yet a little while, and he that shall come will come, and will not tarry.

³⁸ Now the just shall live by faith: but if any man draws back, my soul shall have no pleasure in him.

³⁹ But we are not of them who draw back unto perdition; but of them that believe to the saving of the soul.

My faith protects my love, my holiness, my worship and my anointing and my properties.

It is my duty and my responsibility to speak continually of faith, to share faith, to swallow faith, to digest faith, to meditate faith. Wherever I am in any situation it is a precious task to manifest my faith and the glory of God will come to demonstrate the power of the Word.

Faith sees the unseen.

Faith speaks the unseen.

Faith rejects all that are against the Word of God.

The basic elements of faith are hope and belief that create a guarantee based on the promises of God.

Faith is now, not another time. Use faith now in the present situation.

Faith chases away fear and doubt.

Faith is an act of obedience to all spoken words of God.

Faith is not hope though it contains hope.

Faith creates hope and joy for what we expect, believing the Word of God and His promise.

Abraham believed God without a material sign but he created inside him a real hope of expectation that God demonstrated by presenting a ram of sacrifice instead of Isaac, Abraham's son.

Faith fights all fleshly reactions and doesn't have a spare room for all pagan litany and imaginations.

To handle this process we have to exercise our faith each day and each hour wherever we may be.

Therefore, faith is a daily discipline not only for one day or on a special occasion. It is a discipline throughout our lives and then the nature of God will be in our lives manifesting what Jesus restored to the church.

Faith inspires faith and God is the rewarder of those who use faith.

Faith takes what others cannot take and sees what others cannot see because faith sees the unseen.

Faith causes us to thank God for things that our natural eyes can't see.

Faith creates supernatural realities everywhere using a spiritual language escorted by the Word of God.

All Israel and King Saul feared a man who was insulting them and their God, but a young man without experience in war believed God.

David changed the natural into the supernatural by his faith and boldness. He used the name of Jehovah and words full of great expectation of God's victory.

People thought that he would die, but that opportunity provoked his great elevation in the country. He didn't have a familiar weapon but he knew that he should use the sword of his adversary to remove his head.

Because of a young man who believed God, the sorrows of many days were turned into great joy for people in Israel; the head of Goliath was cut off by an unknown personality. Never mind, by your faith the mountain before you shall be removed. I believe that according to the expectation I have in faith, I will transform my trials into great victories. I shall have what nobody hopes to receive because I create a position by faith and it is mine. Glory to God. I shall not die but I shall proclaim the wonders of God to generations. I believe and I receive (1 Samuel 17).

Faith always sees good things and proclaims them, believing that only God can change any situation to our favor.

Faith sees victory not based on carnal power but by considering the power of God in all circumstances.

Faith is the substance that God uses to bring the unseen to visible eyes.

According the Word of God we are capable of producing fruits by faith.

I believe, then I see. My conversation is not based on what I see but what I believe. I believe that the Word of God is true even when we pass through temptation and trials.

Let God be true and every experience wrong.

Let God be true and all emotions and traditions wrong.

Let God be true and everybody wrong according to Rom 3:4b

As a man thinks in his heart so he is. When Gideon was willing to change the idea that he was coward believing in the word of the angel telling him he was valiant, things changed completely and he won the war (Judges 8).

The same Spirit that raised Jesus from the dead is inside us ready to manifest all that Christ restored to his church.

We have to speak consistently and continually the Word of God and the glory of God will follow us.

As a matter of fact, BELIEVING is to refuse categorically all the lies of the devil.

The devil is a liar and lying is his native language.

Children of God must have a spiritual language composed only by the Word of God.

I confess and declare the Word of God, I resist Satan and I stop all his influences upon you in the name of Jesus.

By confessing with boldness the Word of God I immediately defeat the rulers, the authorities, the powers of this dark world and the spiritual forces of evil in the heavenly realms.

I believe in the supernatural, so to continue to speak the Word I create my own territory where Jesus is controlling all movements and threats.

Jesus is my Lord. I cannot be defeated as I continue to believe and act.

Faith is my clothing and hope is my buttons so there is no place the devil can have access to me when I realize this fact continually.

Greatness is to create a divine and supernatural culture instead of traditions and old stories.

All the blessings of Abraham are mine: so I have the blessing to increase, to subdue and to multiply what Adam lost in Eden.

It is true that by faith I have to carry God's vision in my life and not selfish ambitions; I am predestined to prosper being a son of God.

Tongue has the power of life and death, we have to choose. I choose life and I do not have to deal with the death (Pr 18:21).

Your words can destroy your destiny and your life; the Bible tells us that by your words you will be acquitted and by your words you will be condemned. We have to be very careful (Matt 12:36-37).

Declare right words to yourself, to your wife and to your children and it shall come to pass.

Curse is called banishing and destroying words of blessing, do not curse your life (Pr 6:2). Thou art snared with the words of thy mouth, thou art taken with the words of thy mouth.

When Adam was cursed, all creation was contaminated; man and animal started to kill the earth and human beings experienced a sort of sterility; sickness and disorder appeared. But I praise the Lord, Jesus came to destroy the work of the devil. Nailed on the cross Jesus said, "It is finished." We have to believe this blessing proclaimed by the angel on Luke 2; 9-10 And, lo, the angel of the Lord came upon them, and the glory of the Lord shone round about them: and they were sore afraid.

[10] And the angel said unto them, Fear not: for, behold, I bring you good tidings of great joy, which shall be to all people.

[11] For unto you is born this day in the city of David a Saviour, which is Christ the Lord.

This good news is not only for Jews but to all people, Jesus is the blessing to all the people; He is my blessing, He is your blessing and for all who shall believe in him regardless the race, tribe, color, gender or education.

What I say is what I believe.

What I think is who I am.

The good thing is to have the abundance of the Word of God filling my heart because out of the overflow of my heart my mouth speaks.

2 Cor 4 :13-14,17-18 [13] We having the same spirit of faith, according as it is written, I believed, and therefore have I spoken; we also believe, and therefore speak; [14] Knowing that he which raised up the Lord Jesus shall raise up us also by Jesus, and shall present us with you.

[17] For our light affliction, which is but for a moment, worketh for us a far more exceeding and eternal weight of glory;

[18] While we look not at the things which are seen, but at the things which are not seen: for the things which are seen are temporal; but the things which are not seen are eternal.

Those who are sons and daughters of God have to get the language of faith and the positive confession.

LET'S LEARN A GOOD WAY TO CONFESS AND DECLARE OUR RIGHTS

2 Cor. 10

[3]For though I walk in the flesh, I do not war after the flesh:

[4](For the weapons of our warfare are not carnal, but mighty through God to the pulling down of strongholds;)

[5]Casting down imaginations, and every high thing that exalteth itself against the knowledge of God, and bringing into captivity every thought to the obedience of Christ;

[6]And having in readiness to revenge all disobedience, when My obedience is fulfilled.

King James Version (KJV)

Psalm 23

[1]The LORD is my shepherd; I shall not want.

[2]He maketh me to lie down in green pastures: he leadeth me beside the still waters.

[3]He restoreth my soul: he leadeth me in the paths of righteousness for his name's sake.

[4]Yea, though I walk through the valley of the shadow of death, I will fear no evil: for thou art with me; thy rod and thy staff they comfort me.

[5]Thou preparest a table before me in the presence of mine enemies: thou anointest my head with oil; my cup runneth over.

[6]Surely goodness and mercy shall follow me all the days of my life: and I will dwell in the house of the LORD forever.

Deuteronomy 28

New International Version (NIV)

Blessings for Obedience

[1] Because I obey the LORD My God and carefully follow all his commands He gives me today, the LORD my God will set me high above all the nations on earth. [2] All these blessings will come on me and accompany me because I obey the LORD My God:

[3] I will be blessed in the city and blessed in the country.

[4] The fruit of My womb will be blessed, and the crops of My land and the young of My livestock—the calves of My herds and the lambs of My flocks.

[5] My basket and my kneading trough will be blessed.

[6] I will be blessed when I come in and blessed when I go out.

[7] The LORD will grant that the enemies who rise up against Me will be defeated before Me. They will come at Me from one direction but flee from Me in seven.

[8] The LORD will send a blessing on My barns and on everything I put My hand to. The LORD My God will bless Me in the land he is giving Me.

[9] The LORD will establish Me as his holy people, as he promised Me on oath, if I keep the commands of the LORD My God and walk in obedience to him. [10] Then all the peoples on earth will see that I am called by the name of the LORD, and they will fear Me. [11] The LORD will grant Me abundant prosperity—in the fruit of My womb, the young of My livestock and the crops of My ground—in the land he swore to my ancestors to give me.

[12] The LORD will open the heavens, the storehouse of his bounty, to send rain on your land in season and to bless all the work of my hands. I will lend to many nations but will borrow from none. [13] The LORD will make Me the head, not the tail. I pay attention to the commands of the LORD My God that He gives Me this day and carefully follow them, I will always be at the top, never at the bottom. [14] Do not turn aside from any of the commands He gives Me today, to the right or to the left, following other gods and serving them.

Psalm 103

[8] The LORD is merciful and gracious, slow to anger, and plenteous in mercy.

[9] He will not always chide: neither will he keep his anger forever.

[10] He hath not dealt with us after our sins; nor rewarded us according to our iniquities.

[11] For as the heaven is high above the earth, so great is his mercy toward them that fear him.

[12] As far as the east is from the west, so far hath he removed our transgressions from us.

[13] Like as a father pitieth his children, so the LORD pitieth them that fear him.

[14] For he knoweth our frame; he remembereth that we are dust.

The Lord knows our frame and it is because of his mercy that we succeed.

We are sons and daughters of God. We are his property. We are the hammer of war and through us God will knock holes in the Enemy's lines for His glory.

"I am a new creation, I am created in righteousness and true holiness. I am blameless in Christ. I am sanctified and set apart for God. God lives inside of me. And "greater is He that is in me than he that is in the world." Christ is my wisdom, redemption, sanctification, and righteousness." -Ian Taylor

I will praise The Lord who is my God.

The Lord is my redeemer.

He is my deliverer.

He is my hope.

He is the rock of my salvation.

The Lord purified me.

The Lord sanctified me.

The Lord is with me.

I dwell in His presence.

I have the divine protection.

He is my provider.

He is my source of joy.

He healed me totally.

He forgave all my sins.

He restores my soul.

His goodness and mercy shall escort me all the days of my life.

I shall not die but I shall live for the glory of God.

I am the living tabernacle of God and the cloud of the glory of God is upon me.

God anointed me to preach the gospel, to heal the sick, to open the eyes of the blind.

Miracles are mine, blessings are mine, healing is mine.

God opened a door of success to me that nobody can close.

God is the creator and the doer of wonders and signs.

Nothing is impossible to God. God is here; the glory of God is here.

God will never forget me.

God will give me more than seven elevations; seven blessings, seven promotions.

With my hand I will touch the goodness of God. With my eyes I shall see wonders and signs to my favor.

I am more than a conqueror; I am the hammer and instrument of war for God.

I can do all things through God who strengthens me.

Heaven is mine, holiness is mine, and fresh anointing is mine. Money will follow me and God will multiply my seed.

Increase is mine, victory is mine.

I am in the presence of God; I am in the glory of God.

No weapon formed against me shall prosper. Jesus is the same yesterday, today and forever.

Boldness is mine, I believe in the supernatural and no devil will stand before me.

God will give me a good end.

God will make all my projects to come true. Miracle, signs, wonders shall follow me.

God will make my name great and I always will be above and never beneath all the days of my life.

God will put me in a high position and my enemies will come to kneel before my God.

My seeds will come to God and to me and no more family disappointments in Jesus' name.

I have the revelation of God and the Holy Spirit is inside me.

I HAVE WON IN JESUS' NAME

Psalm 91

[2]I will say of the LORD, He is my refuge and my fortress: my God; in him will I trust.

[3]Surely he shall deliver Me from the snare of the fowler, and from the noisome pestilence.

[4]He shall cover Me with his feathers, and under his wings shalt I trust: his truth shall be My shield and buckler.

[5]I shalt not be afraid for the terror by night; nor for the arrow that flieth by day;

[6]Nor for the pestilence that walketh in darkness; nor for the destruction that wasteth at noonday.

[7]A thousand shall fall at My side, and ten thousand at My right hand; but it shall not come nigh Me.

[8]Only with Mine eyes shalt I behold and see the reward of the wicked.

[9]Because I hast made the LORD, which is my refuge, even the most High, My habitation;

[10]There shall no evil befall Me, neither shall any plague come nigh My dwelling.

[11]For He shall give his angels charge over Me, to keep Me in all thy ways.

I am more than a conqueror; the power of God will enable me to reach beyond my expectation. The angel of God's camp is within my compound, protecting both me and all my belongings. I am blessed, though I may see the opposite, because I walk by faith and not by sight. God will give me the ability to fulfill all my dreams. I am what God says I am and my title is not based on what the people think but what God is planning for me. They will fight me but they will not win over me.

God will make my name great. Genesis 12 [2]And I will make of thee a great nation, and I will bless thee, and make thy name great; and thou shalt be a blessing:

God said that whatsoever I do shall prosper. Psalm 1; [1]Blessed is the man that walketh not in the counsel of the ungodly, nor standeth in the way of sinners, nor sitteth in the seat of the scornful.

[2]But his delight is in the law of the LORD; and in his law doth he meditate day and night.

[3]And he shall be like a tree planted by the rivers of water, that bringeth forth his fruit in his season; his leaf also shall not wither; and whatsoever he doeth shall prosper.

God said I shall be always above and not beneath: Deuteronomy 28; [13]And the LORD shall make thee the head, and not the tail; and thou shalt be above only, and thou shalt not be beneath; if that thou hearken unto the commandments of the LORD thy God, which I command thee this day, to observe and to do them:

God said that He is my help and my refuge in time of trouble. Psalm 46 [1]God is our refuge and strength, a very present help in trouble.

[2]Therefore will not we fear, though the earth be removed, and though the mountains be carried into the midst of the sea;

God has my promotion in mind. Psalm75 [6]For promotion cometh neither from the east, nor from the west, nor from the south.

[7]But God is the judge: he putteth down one, and setteth up another

God said I have to remind or reason with him. Isaiah1; [18]Come now, and let us reason together, saith the LORD: though your sins be as scarlet, they shall be as white as snow; though they be red like crimson, they shall be as wool.

[19]If ye be willing and obedient, ye shall eat the good of the land:

God said He will protect me over water and over fire. Isaiah 43 [1]But now thus saith the LORD that created thee, O Jacob, and he that formed thee, O Israel, Fear not: for I have redeemed thee, I have called thee by thy name; thou art mine.

[2]When thou passest through the waters, I will be with thee; and through the rivers, they shall not overflow thee: when thou walkest through the fire, thou shalt not be burned; neither shall the flame kindle upon thee.

God said his word will not return void but shall accomplish his purpose. Isaiah 55 [8]For my thoughts are not your thoughts, neither are your ways my ways, saith the LORD.

[9]For as the heavens are higher than the earth, so are my ways higher than your ways, and my thoughts than your thoughts.

[10]For as the rain cometh down, and the snow from heaven, and returneth not thither, but watereth the earth, and maketh it bring forth and bud, that it may give seed to the sower, and bread to the eater:

[11]So shall my word be that goeth forth out of my mouth: it shall not return unto me void, but it shall accomplish that which I please, and it shall prosper in the thing whereto I sent it.

God said that no weapon formed against me shall prosper. Isaiah 54 [17]No weapon that is formed against thee shall prosper; and every tongue that shall rise against thee in judgment thou shalt condemn. This is the heritage of the servants of the LORD, and their righteousness is of me, saith the LORD.

God said that I shall not give him rest till He establish my justice. Isaiah 62 [5]For as a young man marrieth a virgin, so shall thy sons marry thee: and as the bridegroom rejoiceth over the bride, so shall thy God rejoice over thee.

[6]I have set watchmen upon thy walls, O Jerusalem, which shall never hold their peace day nor night: ye that make mention of the LORD, keep not silence,

[7]And give him no rest, till he establish, and till he make Jerusalem a praise in the earth.

[8]The LORD hath sworn by his right hand, and by the arm of his strength, Surely I will no more give thy corn to be meat for thine enemies; and the sons of the stranger shall not drink thy wine, for the which thou hast labored:

God said He knew me while I was in the womb of my mother and He consecrated me, giving me an order to destroy the kingdom of the devil and to build and plant his kingdom. Jeremiah 1 [4]Then the word of the LORD came unto me, saying,

[5]Before I formed thee in the belly I knew thee; and before thou camest forth out of the womb I sanctified thee, and I ordained thee a prophet unto the nations.

[6]Then said I, Ah, Lord GOD! behold, I cannot speak: for I am a child.

[7]But the LORD said unto me, Say not, I am a child: for thou shalt go to all that I shall send thee, and whatsoever I command thee thou shalt speak.

[8]Be not afraid of their faces: for I am with thee to deliver thee, saith the LORD.

[9]Then the LORD put forth his hand, and touched my mouth. And the LORD said unto me, Behold, I have put my words in thy mouth.

[10]See, I have this day set thee over the nations and over the kingdoms, to root out, and to pull down, and to destroy, and to throw down, to build, and to plant.

God said they will fight me but they will not win over me; Jeremiah [19]And they shall fight against thee; but they shall not prevail against thee; for I am with thee, saith the LORD, to deliver thee.

God said He has thoughts of peace toward me; Jeremiah 29; [11]For I know the thoughts that I think toward you, saith the LORD, thoughts of peace, and not of evil, to give you an expected end.

¹²Then shall ye call upon me, and ye shall go and pray unto me, and I will hearken unto you.

¹³And ye shall seek me, and find me, when ye shall search for me with all your heart.

¹⁴And I will be found of you, saith the LORD: and I will turn away your captivity, and I will gather you from all the nations, and from all the places whither I have driven you, saith the LORD; and I will bring you again into the place whence I caused you to be carried away captive.

Mark 16; ¹⁵And he said unto them, Go ye into all the world, and preach the gospel to every creature.

¹⁶He that believeth and is baptized shall be saved; but he that believeth not shall be damned.

¹⁷And these signs shall follow them that believe. In my name shall they cast out devils; they shall speak with new tongues;

¹⁸They shall take up serpents; and if they drink any deadly thing, it shall not hurt them; they shall lay hands on the sick, and they shall recover.

God said He will not forsake me or forget me. Hebrews 13 ⁵Let your conversation be without covetousness; and be content with such things as ye have: for he hath said, I will never leave thee, nor forsake thee.

⁶So that we may boldly say, the Lord is my helper, and I will not fear what man shall do unto me.

⁷Remember them which have the rule over you, who have spoken unto you the Word of God: whose faith follow, considering the end of their conversation.

⁸Jesus Christ the same yesterday, and today, and forever.

The Word of God says nothing is impossible to God. ³⁷For with God nothing shall be impossible.

God has already blessed me; no curse or witches can succeed against me. Number 24 ⁷And he took up his parable, and said, Balak the king of Moab hath brought me from Aram, out of the mountains of the east, saying, Come, curse me Jacob, and come, defy Israel.

⁸How shall I curse whom God hath not cursed? or how shall I defy whom the LORD hath not defied?

⁹For from the top of the rocks I see him, and from the hills I behold him: lo, the people shall dwell alone, and shall not be reckoned among the nations.

¹⁰Who can count the dust of Jacob, and the number of the fourth part of Israel? Let me die the death of the righteous, and let my last end be like his!

God is not a man to lie or a son of man to repent. Number 23 [19]God is not a man, that he should lie; neither the son of man, that he should repent: hath he said, and shall he not do it? or hath he spoken, and shall he not make it good?

[20]Behold, I have received commandment to bless: and he hath blessed; and I cannot reverse it.

[21]He hath not beheld iniquity in Jacob, neither hath he seen perverseness in Israel: the LORD his God is with him, and the shout of a king is among them.

[22]God brought them out of Egypt; he hath as it were the strength of an unicorn.

[23]Surely there is no enchantment against Jacob, neither is there any divination against Israel: according to this time it shall be said of Jacob and of Israel, What hath God wrought!

[24]Behold, the people shall rise up as a great lion, and lift up himself as a young lion: he shall not lie down until he eat of the prey, and drink the blood of the slain.

God said: I am his hammer and an instrument of war. Jeremiah 51 [20]Thou art my battle axe and weapons of war: for with thee will I break in pieces the nations, and with thee will I destroy kingdoms;

[21]And with thee will I break in pieces the horse and his rider; and with thee will I break in pieces the chariot and his rider;

God said that the last glory of this house shall be greater than the first. Haggai 2 [5]According to the word that I covenanted with you when ye came out of Egypt, so my spirit remaineth among you: fear ye not.

[6]For thus saith the LORD of hosts; Yet once, it is a little while, and I will shake the heavens, and the earth, and the sea, and the dry land;

[7]And I will shake all nations, and the desire of all nations shall come: and I will fill this house with glory, saith the LORD of hosts.

[8]The silver is mine, and the gold is mine, saith the LORD of hosts.

[9]The glory of this latter house shall be greater than of the former, saith the LORD of hosts: and in this place will I give peace, saith the LORD of hosts.

God has anointed me. Luke 4 [17]And there was delivered unto him the book of the prophet Isaiah. And when he had opened the book, he found the place where it was written,

[18]The Spirit of the Lord is upon me, because he hath anointed me to preach the gospel to the poor; he hath sent me to heal the brokenhearted, to preach deliverance to the captives, and recovering of sight to the blind, to set at liberty them that are bruised,

[19]To preach the acceptable year of the Lord.

God told me to ask him. Matt 7 [7]Ask, and it shall be given you; seek, and ye shall find; knock, and it shall be opened unto you:

⁸For every one that asketh, receiveth; and he that seeketh, findeth; and to him that knocketh it shall be opened.

⁹Or what man is there of you, whom if his son ask bread, will he give him a stone?

¹⁰Or if he ask a fish, will he give him a serpent?

¹¹If ye then, being evil, know how to give good gifts unto your children, how much more shall your Father which is in heaven give good things to them that ask him?

¹²Therefore all things whatsoever ye would that men should do to you, do ye even so to them: for this is the law and the prophets.

God is pleased to release mercy. Matt 9 ¹²But when Jesus heard that, he said unto them, They that be whole need not a physician, but they that are sick.

¹³But go ye and learn what that meaneth, I will have mercy, and not sacrifice: for I am not come to call the righteous, but sinners to repentance.

God gave me the power to chase demons. Matt 10 ¹And when he had called unto him his twelve disciples, he gave them power against unclean spirits, to cast them out, and to heal all manner of sickness and all manner of disease. ⁷And as ye go, preach, saying, The kingdom of heaven is at hand.

⁸Heal the sick, cleanse the lepers, raise the dead, cast out devils: freely ye have received, freely give.

God said whoever receives me is receiving Him and he shall have a reward. Matthew 10 ⁴⁰He that receiveth you receiveth me, and he that receiveth me receiveth him that sent me.

⁴¹He that receiveth a prophet in the name of a prophet shall receive a prophet's reward; and he that receiveth a righteous man in the name of a righteous man shall receive a righteous man's reward.

⁴²And whosoever shall give to drink unto one of these little ones a cup of cold water only in the name of a disciple, verily I say unto you, he shall in no wise lose his reward. God said that his kingdom is for those who desire it violently. Matt 11 ¹²And from the days of John the Baptist until now the kingdom of heaven suffereth violence, and the violent take it by force.

God said if I believe nothing shall be impossible to me. Matt 17 ¹⁹Then came the disciples to Jesus apart, and said, Why could not we cast him out?

²⁰And Jesus said unto them, Because of your unbelief: for verily I say unto you, If ye have faith as a grain of mustard seed, ye shall say unto this mountain, Remove hence to yonder place; and it shall remove; and nothing shall be impossible unto you.

²¹Howbeit this kind goeth not out but by prayer and fasting.

God gave me the power to march on the scorpion and on all the power of the devil and nothing shall harm me. (Luke 10) [18]And he said unto them, I beheld Satan as lightning fall from heaven.

[19]Behold, I give unto you power to tread on serpents and scorpions, and over all the power of the enemy: and nothing shall by any means hurt you.

The Word of God challenges me to be able to do all things having the power of God. Philippians 4:[13]I can do all things through Christ which strengtheneth me.

1 Peter 2 [9]But We are a chosen generation, a royal priesthood, an holy nation, a peculiar people; that ye should shew forth the praises of him who hath called Us out of darkness into his marvellous light;

[10]Which in time past were not a people, but are now the people of God: which had not obtained mercy, but now have obtained mercy.

[10] Finally, I am strong in the Lord and in his mighty power. [11] Putting on the full armor of God, so that I can take My stand against the devil's schemes. [12] For our struggle is not against flesh and blood, but against the rulers, against the authorities, against the powers of this dark world and against the spiritual forces of evil in the heavenly realms. [13] Therefore putting on the full armor of God, so that when the day of evil comes, I may be able to stand My ground, and after I have done everything, to stand. [14] [1]Stand firm then, with the belt of truth buckled around My waist, with the breastplate of righteousness in place, [15] and with My feet fitted with the readiness that comes from the gospel of peace. [16] In addition to all this, take up the shield of faith, with which I can extinguish all the flaming arrows of the evil one. [17] Taking the helmet of salvation and the sword of the Spirit, which is the word of God.

Faith without works is dead; James : What doth it profit, my brethren, though a man say he hath faith, and have not works? can faith save him?

[15] If a brother or sister be naked, and destitute of daily food,

[16] And one of you say unto them, Depart in peace, be ye warmed and filled; notwithstanding ye give them not those things which are needful to the body; what doth it profit?

[17] Even so faith, if it hath not works, is dead, being alone.

[18] Yea, a man may say, Thou hast faith, and I have works: shew me thy faith without thy works, and I will shew thee my faith by my works.

[19] Thou believest that there is one God; thou doest well: the devils also believe, and tremble.

[20] But wilt thou know, O vain man, that faith without works is dead?

²¹ Was not Abraham our father justified by works, when he had offered Isaac his son upon the altar?

²² Seest thou how faith wrought with his works, and by works was faith made perfect?

²³ And the scripture was fulfilled which saith, Abraham believed God, and it was imputed unto him for righteousness: and he was called the Friend of God.

²⁴ Ye see then how that by works a man is justified, and not by faith only.

III
HOLINESS

1 Cor 3

¹⁶ Know ye not that ye are the temple of God, and that the Spirit of God dwelleth in you?

¹⁷ If any man defile the temple of God, him shall God destroy; for the temple of God is holy, which temple ye are.

¹⁸ Let no man deceive himself. If any man among you seemeth to be wise in this world, let him become a fool, that he may be wise.

¹⁹ For the wisdom of this world is foolishness with God. For it is written, He taketh the wise in their own craftiness.

Holiness is the character of God.

God wants his people to dwell in holiness, here we do not try but we were born in it when we received the Lord Jesus. All become new by receiving the nature of God.

This means that we have to walk in purity of heart. It is our responsibility to keep our hearts pure, our mouths pure, our bodies pure, and our eyes pure.

Therefore we have to avoid any occasion that can defile the nature of God in us.

Our houses must be a place to the presence of God and not a casino where everything can be done or perpetrated inside, except those which go with our faith. A good Christian cannot authorize alcohol, cigarettes, and drugs to enter into his house.

Many Christians do well to not go to the pornographic film theater but unfortunately they have those programs on their televisions.

We have to choose and select good programs for our spiritual and good education rather than all that can defile our hearts and spirits.

What we see and what we hear have a significant impact in our lives. Better to pay attention to it.

The dress of sexual immorality is another way of seduction; Christians have to wear the clothes that cover their bodies. If the way you dress can attract anybody to sexual feeling, you become the door of perversion. Be holy in all your behaviors.

Christians have to exercise pure language, not speaking insults and profanity and lies. There are many jokes that produce quarrels and conflicts; better to avoid them.

Do not defile your mouth by profanity that uses the world, we are not of this world even though we live temporally on earth.

Be very careful to not allow your words and your look to be the points of seduction and temptation.

All wrong purposes you have in all that you are doing is called a sin.

Leviticus [20]

[26] And ye shall be holy unto me: for I the LORD am holy, and have severed you from other people, that ye should be mine.

You do not have the right to displace or to take anything that doesn't belong to you; this is to steal, no matter the importance.

Ask permission; ask every time you want to use what belongs to others.

Pay honestly and within a reasonable time all that you borrowed. If you are not ready for just cause please apologize in good time. Do not be a slave of bad habits.

Using many words to justify yourself when you are wrong are a sin and a source of the lie. We have to recognize our debts even when there is no witness or documents.

Because of this, many Christians will not see God. I know pastors who took my books yet refuse to pay me. I was shocked, not because of the money, but because they closed the door to enter into heaven if they do not repent. I tried to convince them through their elders in a polite way. They said what they wanted to defile my person. This is a sad action that resists God in our deeds.

Selfishness is another door of sin. What is not your right, how can you continue to discuss it? You want to falsify things to find a reason for your selfish action. Know that on top of all, God will judge you; better to repent and give back what doesn't belong to you.

Our agreement to anybody shall be respected so we will walk closely with God in all we are doing. Integrity and faithfulness always have a good end.

Luke 16

[10] He that is faithful in that which is least is faithful also in much: and he that is unjust in the least is unjust also in much.

Holiness means that I resemble God's character in my life and I hate the sinful nature.

Ephesians 5

[3] But fornication, and all uncleanness, or covetousness, let it not be once named among you as becometh saints;

[4] Neither filthiness, nor foolish talking, nor jesting, which are not convenient: but rather giving of thanks.

⁵ For this ye know, that no whoremonger, nor unclean person, nor covetous man, who is an idolater, hath any inheritance in the kingdom of Christ and of God.

⁶ Let no man deceive you with vain words: for because of these things cometh the wrath of God upon the children of disobedience.

⁷ Be not ye therefore partakers with them.

⁸ For ye were sometimes darkness, but now are ye light in the Lord: walk as children of light:

⁹ (For the fruit of the Spirit is in all goodness and righteousness and truth;)

¹⁰ Proving what is acceptable unto the Lord.

¹¹ And have no fellowship with the unfruitful works of darkness, but rather reprove them.

¹² For it is a shame even to speak of those things which are done of them in secret.

¹³ But all things that are reproved are made manifest by the light: for whatsoever doth make manifest is light.

¹⁴ Wherefore he saith, Awake thou that sleepest, and arise from the dead, and Christ shall give thee light.

¹⁵ See then that ye walk circumspectly, not as fools, but as wise,

¹⁶ Redeeming the time, because the days are evil.

¹⁷ Wherefore be ye not unwise, but understanding what the will of the Lord is.

¹⁸ And be not drunk with wine, wherein is excess; but be filled with the Spirit;

¹⁹ Speaking to yourselves in psalms and hymns and spiritual songs, singing and making melody in your heart to the Lord;

²⁰ Giving thanks always for all things unto God and the Father in the name of our Lord Jesus Christ;

²¹ Submitting yourselves one to another in the fear of God.

²² Wives, submit yourselves unto your own husbands, as unto the Lord.

²³ For the husband is the head of the wife, even as Christ is the head of the church: and he is the saviour of the body.

I beseech you my brothers and sisters to avoid the culture of drunkenness, a child of God and especially a minister has to be separated from alcoholism.

This is a big door that Satan uses to destroy and to defile those who use it; please children of God, reject this unholy mentality.

Lev 10

9 Do not drink wine nor strong drink, thou, nor thy sons with thee, when ye go into the tabernacle of the congregation, lest ye die: it shall be a statute for ever throughout your generations:

¹⁰ And that ye may put difference between holy and unholy, and between unclean and clean;

[11] And that ye may teach the children of Israel all the statutes which the LORD hath spoken unto them by the hand of Moses.

IV
TRUE WORSHIP

John 4

[21] "Woman," Jesus replied, "believe me, a time is coming when you will worship the Father neither on this mountain nor in Jerusalem. [22] You Samaritans worship what you do not know; we worship what we do know, for salvation is from the Jews. [23] Yet a time is coming and has now come when the true worshipers will worship the Father in the Spirit and in truth, for they are the kind of worshipers the Father seeks. [24] God is spirit, and his worshipers must worship in the Spirit and in truth."

I.   INTRODUCTION

To worship The Lord is our first responsibility. In our prayers we are dealing with our concern. In thanksgiving, we are dealing with our blessings; but in adoration, God is the focus of our attention. When we worship the Lord we first look to rejoice and to satisfy the heart of our heavenly Father.

God is looking for not the preacher or the intercessors but the true worshippers. The ministry of the gospel is for the sinners to receive Jesus. The first responsibility of the pastor is to make this new converter to be a true worshipper.

Adoration is the first thing and follows the service Matt 4: 10: "Worship the Lord your God, and serve Him only."

God never plans to make a new believer immediately his minister, but He delights that the young member becomes a worshipper.

God created us for himself, we have to handle this practice of worshipping the Lord and make it our spiritual culture.

According to Ephesians 1: 12 we were predestined to live by celebrating his glory. Our first ministry is to worship God.

II.   THE DIFFERENCE BETWEEN WORSHIP AND PRAISE.

We worship God as He is, manifesting interior and exterior signs (to kneel down and to bow to give honor and strong respect to God showing the fear of God).

Adoration means to love exceedingly, to honor; to admire; to magnify; to glorify making an act of spiritual communion.

III. DEFINITION OF PRAISE AND WORSHIP

1. <u>Definition of Adoration</u>

Three words are used in the Old Testament for adoration

1. **Segad: means to bow down, manifesting a great fear and a great respect.**
2. **Abad: it generally means "to work" or to serve God.**
3. **Shakah: It is the familiar word used in the Old Testament. It describes a specific act of adoration, "to bow down," to kneel ourselves to give homage and honor." It reflects a deep love and a great humility.**

In other words, Adoration is to manifest the reverence, to have a great fear mixed with respect, it means to kneel down with ardent love, to submit and obey the person whom we love with passion.

In the New Testament we also have three familiar words for adoration.

1. **Seboumai: This means "great fear," "a deep respect," "and an unlimited admiration." These feelings of holy fear have a role important in adoration.**
2. **Latreno: which means "to serve," corresponds to the condition of the servant or a slave; to serve God means also to adore Him.**
3. **Proskuneo: corresponds to the Hebraic word Shakah. Often used in the New Testament, it means "to bow down and to kiss the hand."**

We may bow down to somebody who can be a long distance from us, but for kissing the hand of the master, it requires an intimate personal contact with him. To adore means "to bow down and to kiss the hand."

In general all that we do to the Lord and all that we bring to Him is the act of adoration.

The adoration proceeds from a heart that loves God with passion, in a holy fear and a deep admiration.

The Lord Jesus knew that these two aspects in adoration are very important. However, all our lives must be infected with adoration.

Tempted by the devil who claimed his adoration, the Lord replied severely "you shall adore (Proskuneo) the Lord your God, and to serve Him alone (Latreno, Luke 4: 8).

2. <u>**Definition of Praise**</u>

1. **"ALLELUAH"** Hebrew word that means "Praise the Lord." This is the familiar word often used to express praise.

The word" Hallal "means precisely: celebrate, glorify, to boast, to be passionate, to glorify and to be strongly enthusiastic. It is the expression of an extraordinary explosion of great joy in the act of praise. It is somewhat similar to what a sport fan feels just 15 seconds before the end of the competition when his favorite team will win. If he is a true supporter he will stand lifting his hands and shout for victory. It is exactly what the word "Hallal" is.

Therefore, we shall praise the Lord, glorify Him for his exploits and signify his grandeur with a powerful enthusiasm in the way that other people can think we are made. A person who praises God in this way feels a deep love in his heart for the Lord. This doesn't mean that we act like we're mad but those who surround us may think that we are mad (Psalm 84 : 4 -6). [4] Blessed are they that dwell in thy house: they will be still praising thee. Selah.

[5] Blessed is the man whose strength is in thee; in whose heart are the ways of them.

[6] Who passing through the valley of Baca, make it a well; the rain also filleth the pools.

2. **Yadah:** It means to thank the Lord, publicly lifting the hands. In 2 Chronicles 20 when the Levites went in the sight of the army praising the Lord, they said: "Praise (YADAH) the Lord, because his mercy endures forever." When Levites lifted their voices expressing their praises to God, the enemy was destroyed.

[21] And when he had consulted with the people, he appointed singers unto the LORD, and that should praise the beauty of holiness, as they went out before the army, and to say, Praise the LORD; for his mercy endureth for ever.

[22] And when they began to sing and to praise, the LORD set ambushments against the children of Ammon, Moab, and mount Seir, which were come against Judah; and they were smitten.

"Lift your hands in the sanctuary and bless the Lord" (Ps. 134: 2). "Ezra blessed the Lord, the almighty God, and the people replied lifting their hands: Amen! Amen! (Ne 8:6) [5] And Ezra opened the book in the sight of all the people; (for he was above all the people;) and when he opened it, all the people stood up:

[6] And Ezra blessed the LORD, the great God. And all the people answered, Amen, Amen, with lifting up their hands: and they bowed their heads, and worshipped the LORD with their faces to the ground.

To lift your hands is a sign of surrender and love before God. This is the meaning of Yadah. "I will bless you therefore all my life; I will lift my hands at your name" (Ps 63 :4-5).

The Greek word corresponding to Hallal and Yadah in the New Testament is Aineo and means to praise. "And suddenly, a multitude of heavenly army join the angel, praising (Aineo) God" (Luke 2 :13-14) [3] And suddenly there was with the angel a multitude of the heavenly host praising God, and saying,

[14] Glory to God in the highest, and on earth peace, good will toward men.

3. **BARAK: another word of praise means: to bless, to kneel in adoration. To bow down before somebody, manifesting humility and to recognize the superiority and dignity of that person. Barak is therefore to bless.**

In Christ we are blessed in every way spiritually in heavenly places (Ep 1 :3). We bless the Lord (Ps 103 :1-2 03). Bless the LORD, O my soul: and all that is within me, bless his holy name.

[2] Bless the LORD, O my soul, and forget not all his benefits:

4. **Zamar: another corresponding Hebrew word means, play an instrument, to sing and to praise. This is a reference of praise interpreted with music instruments (1 Chronicles 16 :9).** [9] Sing unto him, sing psalms unto him, talk ye of all his wondrous works.

The Greek word for Zamar in New Testament is Psallo (Ps 150), which means sing to the Lord with an instrument. Eph. 5:19-20 [19] Speaking to yourselves in psalms and hymns and spiritual songs, singing and making melody in your heart to the Lord;

[20] Giving thanks always for all things unto God and the Father in the name of our Lord Jesus Christ;

5. **Ruah: this word means: shout for joy: the children of Israel do not have any difficulty expressing their joy in their relation with God. 95 O come, let us sing unto the LORD: let us make a joyful noise to the rock of our salvation.**

[2] Let us come before his presence with thanksgiving, and make a joyful noise unto him with psalms.

³ **For the LORD is a great God, and a great King above all gods.**

We also find "Doxa"which means glory in Jn 9:24 and Acts 16:25 an action of expressing our praise with audible voices. The praise in the New Testament was verbal, public and enthusiastic.

²⁴ **Then again called they the man that was blind, and said unto him, Give God the praise**

ACT 16: 25 ²⁵ And at midnight Paul and Silas prayed, and sang praises unto God: and the prisoners heard them.

The Purpose of Our Worship of God, THE INTERACTIVE BIBLE

The purpose of our worship is to glorify, honor, praise, exalt, and please God. Our worship must show our adoration and loyalty to God for His grace in providing us with the way to escape the bondage of sin, so we can have the salvation He so much wants to give us. The nature of the worship God demands is the prostration of our souls before Him in humble and contrite submission. James 4:6, 10 tells us, "God resists the proud, but gives grace to the humble. **Humble yourselves** in the sight of the Lord, and He will lift you up." Our worship to God is a very humble and reverent action.

Jesus says in John 4:23-24, "But the hour is coming, and now is, **when true worshippers will worship the Father in spirit and in truth,** for the Father is seeking such to worship Him. God is a spirit and they that worship Him **must worship Him in spirit and in truth.**

Our very best in worship is due God and is prescribed by Him in the Bible. The worship God has prescribed is the only way we can be pleasing to Him in this life and finally attain everlasting life with Him in eternity. The Christian's worship is of the greatest importance.

Worship is a time when we pay deep, sincere, awesome respect, love, and fear to the one who created us. Acts 17:24-25 says, "God who made the world and everything in it, since He is Lord of heaven and earth, does not dwell in temples made with hands, as though He needed anything, since He gives life, breath, and all things."

God is the one who holds our eternal destiny in His hands. Philippians 2:12 tells us to "work out your own salvation **with fear and trembling.**"Our salvation is a very serious matter and will not happen by accident. We must work it out "with fear and trembling." Our salvation depends on whether our worship is pleasing to God or not. On the Day of Judgment it will be too late to make any corrections.

Worship should cause us to reflect on the majesty and graciousness of God and Christ, contrasted to our own unworthiness. God does not have to have our worship, but we must worship Him to please Him. Our singing, praying, studying His Word, giving, and communion are designed by God to bring us closer to Him and to cause us to think more like He thinks, thus becoming more like Him. James 4:8 tells us to, "Draw near to God and He will draw near to you."

Our worship not only honors and magnifies God, but it is also for our own edification and strength. Worship helps us develop a God-like and Christ-like character. We become like unto those we admire and worship. When we worship God we tend to value what God values and gradually take on the characteristics and qualities of God, but never to His level. As Philippians 2:5 says, "Let this mind be in you which was also in Christ."How do we take on the mind of Christ? In Romans 12:2 we read, "And do not be conformed to this world, but be transformed by the renewing of your mind." We renew our minds as we study and meditate on God's Word and worship Him.

When we worship God we develop such traits as forgiveness, tenderness, justice, righteousness, purity, kindness, and love. All of this is preparing us for eternal life in heaven with God and Christ. As we are told in Colossians 3:2: "Set your mind on things above, and not on things on the earth."

V
FRESH ANOINTING

I.   The impact of the anointing

1.   **The anointing breaks the yoke**
2.   **The anointing attracts people to hear you the longer you are speaking. The anointing of The Lord made 4000 people to listen to him over three days nights and days without eating (Mark 8: 2-3). The anointing of Paul caused people to hear him all through the night to the morning (Act 20: 7-12). Your anointing will cause people to support your message.**
3.   **The anointing touches directly the Spirit**
4.   **The anointing provokes the joy of the Lord**
5.   **The anointing facilitates people to understand the message.**
6.   **The anointing gives courage and strong power to the preacher**
7.   **The anointing convinces people to repent and to give**

NB: The way many preachers are ministering with a wrong anointing cannot fulfill the Word of God. They have a style of preaching that entertains people rather than to

touch the heart so they may repent. They give false prophecy to demonstrate the power by making people to fall by pushing them. This is not the work of the Holy Spirit but the lie of the devil. I warn the church of God to discern the will of God in all they are accepting--actions that feed only the flesh and not the Spirit. A powerful minister used by the power of the Spirit doesn't force anything, but the demons cry at his presence and by his command he chases them in the name of Jesus. I am very choked up to see the lies practiced by many ministers who think they've found a simple way to get a name and money. We must be very careful; they memorize certain verses of blessing and deliverance without reading the full context of the Word. For example by taking only a portion in Deuteronomy 28 they conclude: "if you obey…" and claim it you will get the superiority over all the nations of the earth and the blessings so on and so on…" this is not true. We have first to obey the voice of God and fulfill all his commands to inherit these blessings.

Children of God, we must be very careful in these last days. Many false prophets are working using what they can to seduce.

II. Now is a good time to break by faith any kind of yoke in Jesus 'name

<u>The anointing shall break the yoke</u>
Isaiah 10: 27

No matter the origin of the yoke, it shall be destroyed by the power of God

No matter the time of bondage, it shall be destroyed.

Whether it comes from the natural or the supernatural it all must be destroyed in Jesus' name.

No more bondage in the name of Jesus, no more turn-around in the name of Jesus.

No more place of defeat in the army of the Lord, because all power has been given to Jesus in heaven and in earth and under the earth.

We cannot be intimidated by names; there is only one powerful name above all names.

Don't be intimidated by any situation, God is in control – don't be intimidated by fear, Jesus won for us (Ps 46: 2-3).

Don't be intimidated by false accusation, Jesus already justifies us.

We are free by divine decree, we are not the same by the power of God, and we are new creatures.

When the Spirit leads us, we are above the natural and what we say by faith is very powerful to shake the heaven and the earth.

The Lord gave us the power to trample on the scorpion and on the serpent and on all the power of the enemy and nothing shall harm us (Luke 10, 18-19).

We are in the good place, a good territory protected by God, secured by heavenly power.

The yoke shall be destroyed.

I have the mandate to root out, and to pull down, and to destroy, and to throw down, to build, and to plant (Jer1: 10).

Now is the time

Now is the appointed moment

Not tomorrow

Not yesterday

But now, now in the name of Jesus

Power is here

The presence of God is here

The blessing is here

The deliverance is here

The healing is here

The miracle we've awaited for so long is here.

Believe and receive in the power of the Holy Spirit.

God is not a man, that he should lie, neither the son of man

that he should repent; what he said, he will make it…

(Num 23:19).

The yoke shall be destroyed ISAIAH 10

²⁷ And it shall come to pass in that day, that his burden shall be taken away from off thy shoulder, and his yoke from off thy neck, and the yoke shall be destroyed because of the anointing.

Everything in the hand of God receives transformation:

A stick becomes a serpent

A stick opens a road in the sea

A stick produces a fountain of water from a rock

Moses becomes extraordinary in the sight of pharaoh.

Anything in the hand of God becomes wonderful

Abnormal becomes normal

Natural becomes supernatural

The worst becomes excellent

No more, no more the same in the hand of God, and I am in the hand of God, I am an overcomer, surely the yoke shall be destroyed

How come the wind could only bring quail to Israel and not serpents or another kind of inedible bird?

How come the little oil and flour in the hand of God was never exhausted till the end of the famine in the land?

A man in the power of the Holy Spirit becomes a new reality, so people can think they know you but they don't. God himself knows the dimension in which he placed you.

(Matt 28:18-20) All power has been given to me in the heaven and on earth.

If people could seek after biblical verses as they do for money, they will experience the glory of God everywhere; unfortunately they do not have time to read, swallow or digest the Word of God.

This is more worthy than gold and silver; few know this and fewer practice it.

There are opportunities that cannot happen anymore

Abraham, in the presence of people he supposed extraordinary, never took that opportunity for granted

It was a unique occasion--by losing it his destiny would be a mess up.

Don't take for granted any godly occasion in your life.

To have a servant of God around can be a master key of your breakthrough if you believe in the promises of God about receiving them in the Lord's purpose (Matt: 10:41-42).

Don't lose the opportunity by blindness in your heart. Do not judge the servant of God, you are not his judge. If he stands he stands before his Lord and if he falls, his Lord shall revive him, which is not your problem. Just receive him and serve him with a pure heart. After giving him food and drink, please give him a time to give you a Word from God and let him pray for you. Stop with your many words. You will not see him again, stop blah, blah, blah, and give that place to the servant of God.

Don't take for granted the opportunity; you are not sure to get it for the second time.

The people of Gerasenes did not know how to benefit by the presence of Jesus in their location, they prayed him to leave and they lost the opportunity forever (Mark 5:17).

The freedom
The meaning of being free

This means debt free; fear free, problem free; obstacle free, free indeed. It shows that I am no more a slave of anything in my life. Christ delivered us from the curse of the law, making himself a curse… (Gal 3:13). It is for freedom that Jesus delivered us so do not put yourselves again under another kind of slavery (Gal 5:1). Therefore I am not controlled by tradition, by emotion, by routine but by the Holy Spirit. Do not put yourselves again under another kind of slavery.

The curse, sin, and slavery are in the same family; you are limited to do completely the will of God. You are under another power that kills you slowly but surely. You are walking with pain, stress, and depression though Jesus came to deliver us completely from all these aspects. If you still feel these in your life you really need spiritual help. The ability to destroy all these curses is by total submission to the will of God. The curse was entering by the disobedience of Adam following the advice of the deceiver, Satan. And even now, when Satan can have a small access to our lives, we cannot benefit completely from the blessing of the blood of Jesus. Know that by obedience we are blessed by the covenant of the blood but by disobedience we put ourselves under another kind of slavery. A person who is under slavery cannot bring a total deliverance. Either you are a preacher or a pastor; you must submit totally to God and reject all kinds of unfaithfulness. In 2 Peter 2: 19 they promise the freedom while they themselves are slaves of corruption. In fact, everyone is a slave of the one who won him over.

Let's take some illustrations: A woman who doesn't obey or respect her husband, she is under another kind of slavery. She cannot benefit from all the blessings of the covenant. The husband who doesn't love his wife is also under another bond. A child who doesn't respect his parents is under a curse. A minister who has destroyed by rebellion the work of God and disobeyed the order of his spiritual leadership is also under bonds. The Word of God must be in practice in order for everybody to benefit from the blessings of the covenant of the blood of Jesus (John 7:37 and John 8:36).

In the meantime, I have to use a language of freedom full of the Word of God. Know that the Spirit of God is always behind the Word of God to fulfill His purpose. Doubt is not coming from God; it comes from the devil. This is the reason I have to confess what I believe and not what I see. By faith I confess the unseen like my Father God does and it shall come to pass as I declare. The principle of faith is the same: If you confess in your mouth the Lord Jesus and if you believe in your heart that God raised him from the death you shall be saved because in your mouth you confess till the salvation and in your heart you believe unto righteousness. The fruit of the Spirit must fill our hearts and not the acts of sinful nature. Gal 5: 19: LOVE, JOY, PEACE, PATIENCE, KINDNESS, GOODNESS, SELF-CONTROL. There is no law over us if these fruits are constantly in all our reactions and deeds. Only by possessing these fruits can we testify that we are led by the Spirit and we can have the guarantee of being free indeed. We cannot be free when we are not led by the Spirit. Our freedom in Christ is supported by the fruits of the Spirit and in opposition there are sexual immorality, impurity, and debauchery, idolatry, selfish ambition, dissension, witchcraft, hatred, discord, jealousy, fits of rage, factions, envy, drunkenness, orgies, and the like. This is the mark of slavery (Galatians 5).

¹³ For, brethren, ye have been called unto liberty; only use not liberty for an occasion to the flesh, but by love serve one another.

¹⁴ For all the law is fulfilled in one word, even in this; Thou shalt love thy neighbor as thyself.

¹⁵ But if ye bite and devour one another, take heed that ye be not consumed one of another

John 8:31

"If you hold my teaching you are really my disciples-then you will know the truth, and the truth will set you free."

John 8:34

I tell you the truth, everyone who sins is a slave of sin – now a slave has no permanent place in the family, but a son belongs to it forever.

John 8:36 states: So if the Son sets you free, you will be free indeed.

John 8:37b You are ready to kill me because you have no room for my words.

John 8:43 Why is my language not clear to you? Because you are unable to hear what I say. John 8: 44 You belong to your father, the devil, and you want to carry out your father's desire. When he lies, **he speaks his native language…**

Out of your overflow of your heart, your mouth speaks (Matt 12:34).

Pay attention to all you decide to hear, to read, and to see, they are filling your heart without control. The consequence will be heard in your mouth and in your daily vocabulary.

Avoid immoral words, they are defiling you and they are not worthy of the children of God. This is an easy way to stabilize and break the yoke. Save more time to hear the Word of God, also to read it. Fill CDs with the Word in your car, not only songs. Songs cannot replace the Word of God but the Word can compose a faithful song. Other songs are not biblical but just good melody.

Know that: Great men, Great commitments, Great vision, Great assignments, Great hearts—they require courage, patience, perseverance, and determination.

How can you join the army of the almighty with a half commitment? It requires discipline and respect to plan and reach life goals.

The tongue has the power of life and death (**Pr 18:21**).

Do not authorize your fear to be the obstacle to your blessing. You must receive your blessing by faith working through love.

Most of the time Jesus told people "fear not" because he knew the inconvenience of fear.

Jesus succeeded everywhere because He always spoke the Father's word till his crucifixion.

Joshua was told to be strong and very courageous; to be careful to obey the law Moses gave him; to not turn from the word of that book to the right or to the left, that he may be successful wherever he went. Joshua 1:8-9: Do not let this Book of the law depart from your mouth; meditate on it day and night… Then you will be prosperous and successful.……Do not be terrified; do not be discouraged, for the Lord your God will be with you wherever you go.

Fear is the brother of doubt and both are the enemy of your destiny.

Always forget the past and go in the new perspective of faith. We have to cover every hole in us, which can be the obstacle to our blessings.

God wants us to be well, to prosper:

It is well with my soul

It is well with my heart

It is well with my spirit

It is well with my business, my family, my project, my faith.

It is well with my Lord Jesus.

The prosperity in all things is possible by faith and love, and not in any other container.

No weapon formed against you shall prosper. Know for sure that you are a son or daughter of God and the divine protection is with you. Refuse all forms of fear and doubt. Put all kinds of carnal mentality away because it is no longer your culture. You have the culture of holiness and the behavior of boldness. You call things by faith and not by sight; the yoke must go. It shall be destroyed.

As long as people won't recognize the negative side of their old nature they will be considered like animals.

Never mix positive confession and negative. You are destroying your future. Let your mouth bless you and resist all the works of the devil. The tongue has the power to save you or to kill you; choose to voice faith and not fear and doubt.

This body seems to be valued when things are well. In case of terrible disease, you have a bad odor everywhere and nobody may wish to stay near you except your wife or husband or your close relative. There you find that you are nothing and you hate yourself.

This is how people without the blood of Jesus inside have a bad smell before God. When they pray they provoke a dead aroma toward God and he cannot tolerate it. This is called spiritual death. Jesus said "Eloi Eloi lama sabaktani, my Father, my Father why do you forsake me?"

At that time he was covering himself with all our sins. He was smelling bad to God, and the remedy was to die so he could destroy the power of sin and the power of death, and when he resurrected he received a name above all names and all knees shall bow before him and each tongue shall confess that Jesus is Lord.

Without the purification by the blood of Jesus people have the odor of death smelling before God. One solution is to repent so God can hear your prayers. People have to repent and let the blood of Jesus cleanse and sanctify them.

Though you may try everything to make yourself well, it cannot be good before God if Jesus didn't set you free by his own blood. There is no other alternative. The body can deceive you, there will be a time of decay and no one can stay with you. We are awaiting the glorious body, which will never smell bad.

We have the good news

It is a sad thing that most religious people go around with bad news though we are called to bring the good news. The stone has to be removed from the tomb of Lazarus. His sister comes with the bad news, "He has a bad odor; he has been dead for four days." Jesus said "Remove the stone." You have to remove it. The voice of Jesus chased away the odor and the death. Miracles are done by God; it is the reality of God. Martha, Lazarus' own sister, might have caused the lack of a miracle if she had persisted in unbelief (John 11:30-40,43-44). Nobody smelled the odor of death from Lazarus.

Distorted servants report only bad news and this shows the kind of spirit behind them.

Few are those who are based on good news.

This is the reason that they have not the true revelation of the church of Christ.

The Spirit of God is upon me because the Lord anointed me to preach the good news to the poor, proclaim freedom to the captives, to release the oppressed and to proclaim the year of the Lord's favor.

Lu 4:18-19

When you develop a rapport with your brother in faith and you learn that he has fallen into sin, you do not have to criticize him or to hate him or to advertise his sin. The first thing to do is to pray for him and go to see him with the goal to help him to be right.

He deserves more love, more attention, more support, more visitation--this is a special way to touch God.

Here is the good place to show true love and God's character. The shepherding Spirit of God will release the oppressed by the compassion and love you invest in the lamb.

Remember the owner of 100 sheep left 99 and went to look for the lost. When he found it he rejoiced and put it on his neck.

The Elevation Comes from God (Ps 75: 6-7)

Don't expect any elevation from men. They always change; put your trust in God. He shall open doors for you.

The drive to rely on somebody can drive you to depression, desolation and discouragement until it destroys your joy. Be very careful. Don't destroy your destiny because of anybody else, including your relatives.

By your faith and dependence on the fresh, anointing the yoke shall be destroyed. Don't follow the voices of men; follow the voices of God, taking his Word as your guarantee, not anybody elses.

N.B Satan will never congratulate you for all the good works you are doing.

He is the deceiver and a liar. He will continue to show you the negatives in your past. He will always show you your past defeat and failure. Never will he let you know that you are able to succeed. The best you can do is to chase him by resisting all his ideas. Always he will try to give you a guilty conscience. This causes many people continual stress and has even resulted at worst in suicide.

Satan is the author of deception and stress. Do not allow him to cause bitterness in you. This is a poison to your whole body and mind.

Rebuke the devil and he will flee from you. Don't take time to argue with him or to negotiate. Chase him in Jesus' name.

You have to take heart and encourage yourself, pray and pray, not emotional prayers but prayers full of faith and boldness.

When you change the way you think and begin to do right actions, the glory of God shall follow you everywhere.

John 13:14 Now that I, your Lord and teacher, have washed your feet, you should wash one another's feet. I have set you an example that you should do as I have done for you 17

What we need for everybody is to be connected constantly

1. The first thing is to overcome sins and likewise:
2. The way to speak and treat others
3. We have to pray till we become prayer
4. We have to praise till we become praise
5. We have to adore till we become adoration
6. We have to give till we become givers or sponsors
7. We have to consecrate till we become good sacrifices
8. We have to love till we become love

9. We have to sing till we become a song of God
10. We have to preach till we become a messenger of God
11. We have to thank till we become thanksgiving
12. We have to smile till we become a smile

There are miracles everywhere when we are connected. No doubt, no joke, no deception. Who told you that you will die BARREN? Who told you that you are miserable? Who told you that you are already condemned? Roman 10:9-10…. 17 when you confess with your mouth the Lord Jesus and believe in your heart that God raised him from death you shall be saved —mouth, salvation, heart, justice. Avoid the association with unbelief; it will cause you to be disconnected and deactivated. Activate your faith by using correctly the Word of God.

Go your way with the weapons of God--spiritual weapons to conquer the terrible tracks of the devil. Sing a new song. Declare the promises of God. Destroy the stronghold of the devil in your life. Keep faith and boldness.

The yoke shall be destroyed by the anointing.

CHAPTER TWO

One word from God can transform your entire life

7 ELEMENTS WHICH PUT BELIEVERS IN BONDAGE

JOHN 8: 36

[36] So if the Son sets you free, you will be free indeed.

I

<u>WORRIES</u>

Brother and Sisters in the Lord, if we fail to believe each word declared by our God through Jesus, we make Him a liar. The first mountain we have to remove is worry. We have to learn to rely on the power and on the defense and provision of God. Never mind the situation; we are called to obey the Word, to eat the Word, to meditate on the Word and to be part of the Word. Actually we are the disciples of Jesus and what makes us his disciples is not another thing but his words.

Do Not Worry, Matthew 6

[25] "Therefore I tell you, do not worry about your life, what you will eat or drink; or about your body, what you will wear. Is not life more than food, and the body more than clothes? [26] Look at the birds of the air; they do not sow or reap or store away in barns, and yet your heavenly Father feeds them. Are you not much more valuable than they? [27] Can any one of you by worrying add a single hour to your life[e]?

[28] "And why do you worry about clothes? See how the flowers of the field grow. They do not labor or spin. [29]

It is mandatory to take God at his word and rejoice, waiting for his manifestation. Do not tremble because of this and that but commit all things to the Lord and quiet your mouth from words of unbelief.

Matthew 11

²⁸ "Come to me, all you who are weary and burdened, and I will give you rest. ²⁹ Take my yoke upon you and learn from me, for I am gentle and humble in heart, and you will find rest for your souls. ³⁰ For my yoke is easy and my burden is light."

No matter how heavy is the burden, Jesus asked us to carry it: But then when we brought the burden to Him, we left it completely and we departed with good news to tell our neighbor, because this caused a new testimony with which to glorify our God.

Paul and Silas in jail saw the glory of God. The counsel on high made an order to deliver them: An angel came to untie them and to open the door of the jail. Glory to God.

I am so excited and I bless the Lord who made me an heir of the treasure of heaven.

The situation you face today is not for long term; it is for a short time.

Loose your faith to go out and face that situation. You have the favor of the high court, you are not guilty. You are free; go in peace in Jesus' name.

You are healed in His name.

You are saved by believing in Jesus Christ.

When the Son of God makes you free you are free indeed

(John 8:36). So do not sell your freedom, your dignity, your personality, though you pass through the fire. Have faith in God and do not authorize anybody to use you because of material things. If you do, you will be a slave of this man though you can by yourself reach beyond his vision. Why allow anybody else to decide on your destiny? Who is he? If it means to starve—better to do it than to be a slave of somebody. God already delivered us. Don't let yourself get lost in the timeframe of your need for daily bread. Wait on God for his life choices for you. He will eventually reveal to you your destiny.

Do not be surprised when some so-called ministers may tell you are exerting your faith in the wrong direction.

Faith is a process, and action is an achiever. Know that it is personal and not from outside. It is inside you, so nobody can believe in your place. You have to persist till you reach your destination.

Even if things are delayed, it does not mean no; wait by faith till you touch the point of destiny.

The Lord Jesus told his disciples to go across the sea themselves while he went to pray on the mountain.

He knew that they would eventually arrive at the destination, but in the middle of their short voyage, wind and storms disturbed their security and their trip. Jesus was praying. As the night grew darker and stormier, the disciples faced a catastrophic moment.

Suddenly, the Lord came walking on the water; and the disciples thought that it was their end, meeting a ghost.

It was not but it was the time of their deliverance.

We will not go like Peter walking on the water by order of Jesus, but the Lord spoke with the wind knowing that the cause of the storm was the wind.

Immediately, the storm ceased and security was reestablished.

The Lord Jesus is our security no matter what wild river we cross.

Philippians 4

⁴ Rejoice in the Lord always. I will say it again: Rejoice! ⁵ Let your gentleness be evident to all. The Lord is near. ⁶ Do not be anxious about anything, but in every situation, by prayer and petition, with thanksgiving, present your requests to God. ⁷ And the peace of God, which transcends all understanding, will guard your hearts and your minds in Christ Jesus.

⁸ Finally, brothers and sisters, whatever is true, whatever is noble, whatever is right, whatever is pure, whatever is lovely, whatever is admirable—if anything is excellent or praiseworthy—think about such things. ⁹ Whatever you have learned or received or heard from me, or seen in me—put it into practice. And the God of peace will be with you.

God is our refuge and strength, a very present help in trouble.

² Therefore will not we fear, though the earth be removed, and though the mountains be carried into the midst of the sea;

³ Though the waters thereof roar and be troubled, though the mountains shake with the swelling thereof.

⁴ There is a river, the streams whereof shall make glad the city of God, the holy place of the tabernacles of the most High.

⁵ God is in the midst of her; she shall not be moved: God shall help her, and that right early.

⁶ The heathen raged, the kingdoms were moved: he uttered his voice, the earth melted.

⁷ The LORD of hosts is with us; the God of Jacob is our refuge.

PRAYER OF FAITH OVER WORRIES

Father, in the name of Jesus I thank you for the new nature I received through Jesus Christ. I resist all the spirit of worries and self-pity in Jesus' name. I submit all the burden onto Jesus' Christ my Savior and my Lord. I rejoice in the Lord. I have the joy of The Lord in my heart. Satan is the liar. I can never follow his voice. I can never develop fear, worries, and doubt. The battle is not mine; in time of combat Jehovah Sabbaoth fights for me. In time of trouble, Jehovah Shalom is my peace. In time of need Jehovah Jireh is my provision. In time of sickness, Jehovah Rapha is my healing. I take authority in the name of Jesus and I recover my stability in the Holy Spirit by the name of Jesus. Not by might not by power but by my Spirit says the Lord. I am not moved by what I see but by the Word of God. I am the winner by God's decree; the blood of Jesus justifies me. I am created to dwell in the love of God. No more striving, no more jealousy, no more gossip, no more hatred, no more arrogance, no more selfishness, no more fleshly competitions. By faith I am on the top and not beneath. Jesus is my Lord, not worries; I confess that I have the joy and the invulnerability of God in Jesus' name. Amen

WHAT SHALL I DO WHEN I AM DISTRESSED?
Psalm 73: 21-28

1. To encourage myself in the Lord.
2. To go before the Lord by asking for His help.
3. If there is something wrong in my life, be ready to repair by repentance and fixing it.
4. To follow the instruction of the Lord.
5. Not be discouraged by what enemies say.
6. To be concentrated on the way of solving an issue.
7. To have a good attitude even toward your persecutor.
8. Keep your mouth from saying profanity and criticism but organize yourself.
9. Thank God for all details and spend times with him.
10. Be yourself and you will not be condemned. Go ahead with your destiny.

Words of exhortation

1. True information about yourself, nobody knows it but God himself who created you.
2. You do not have to be like others, you are called to be special and should not imitate anybody, be original.
3. God knows the material He fixed in you; He is able to help you to fulfill your destiny when you ask Him your true information.
4. Many people will tell you that you are like them, think like them, but all this talk is not true; you are original and you can do all things in the name of The Lord.

5. The information of God is that you can do everything through Christ who enables you. He is your source. He is your fountain. He is the maker of miracles. He is your redeemer. He is the one who sustains you. He taught you how to fight. Although you were down He relieved you. He lifted you up and sanctified you with the blood of Jesus.

6. The fear that you have will make you unable to speak powerfully; you have to set your fear aside and keep believing God.

7. When God elected you He knew that you were a woman or a man, He knew that you were illiterate, He knew who you are and He trusted you. You have to go with the Word of God using His instructions.

8. Know that all that you fear are humans like you but they activated the power inside them.

9. The future is before you; you shall go to all kinds of persons and speak the oracle of God.

10. Faces make the entire world different; remember that those faces are men, not lions or leopards. The word you bring will change and heal them. Don't be afraid, you are a giver of life, a giver of opportunity, a giver of joy, a giver of salvation, a giver of solutions, a giver of miracles.

11. Because you have the message of God in you, God set nations and kingdoms, to root out and to pull down, to build and to plant.

12. All men of God with authority never look for counsel when they have the precise direction from God.

PSALM 73

[21] Thus my heart was grieved, and I was pricked in my reins.

[22] So foolish was I, and ignorant: I was as a beast before thee.

[23] Nevertheless I am continually with thee: thou hast holden me by my right hand.

[24] Thou shalt guide me with thy counsel, and afterward receive me to glory.

[25] Whom have I in heaven but thee? and there is none upon earth that I desire beside thee.

[26] My flesh and my heart faileth: but God is the strength of my heart, and my portion for ever.

[27] For, lo, they that are far from thee shall perish: thou hast destroyed all them that go a whoring from thee.

[28] But it is good for me to draw near to God: I have put my trust in the Lord God, that I may declare all thy works.

II
THE NEGATIVE CONFESSION

By negative confession, people become the enemies of their destinies: by negative confession you throw your destiny in the trash. By it you curse yourself, your family, your property and your whole being.

The tongue has the power of life in it and also the power of death.

The decision is yours but for me I choose Life and not Death. I choose victory and not defeat. I choose success and not failure. I choose holiness and not sin. I choose faith and not doubt and fear. Fear and doubt are my greatest enemies.

I resist them with all my heart

I want you to know that behind all words, there is a spirit that executes the fruit of our words. Words are strong and by it the world was created. We are created in the image of God; we also create situations by our words. Before we fight we say a word to God and then we fight; before we build we say, "Tomorrow I will start my building." Before all situations comes first the word.

Proverbs 6

New International Version (NIV)

Warnings Against Folly

6 My son, if you have put up security for your neighbor,

if you have shaken hands in pledge for a stranger,

² you have been trapped by what you said,

ensnared by the words of your mouth.

When you say, "It is finished for me! I am defeated!" the devil caught you! "I cannot! I am not...!" You say this experience will kill you...! You are without grace and favor! With these pagan words you are killing yourself and destroying all your projects by your words. Change the way you confess and the change will benefit you.

ROMAN 12 THE POWER OF THE WORD

"The word is near you; it is in your mouth and in your heart,"[d] that is, the message concerning faith that we proclaim: ⁹ If you declare with your mouth, 'Jesus is Lord,' and believe in your heart that God raised him from the dead, you will be saved. ¹⁰ For it is with your heart that you believe and are justified, and it is with your mouth that you profess your faith and are saved. ¹¹ As Scripture says, "Anyone who believes in him will never be put to shame."

Peter in jail, waiting the sentence of death, instead, saw an angel who was ordered by the counsel from above to deliver Him.

The counsel of above is in our favor and not against us so rejoice because of this right.

This is vanity and makes somebody a charlatan.

Be strong in faith and be true and honest in your walk with God.

Sometimes your faith may cause you to pass through the fire but this fire will never consume you (Isaiah 43:2).

These people of Israel who saw great miracles of God neglected him, saying they would surely die in the desert. The spirit behind them made them to die in fulfillment of their words—that is, except Caleb and Joshua and the generation below twenty years of age. But all adults older than twenty were killed in the desert. They ate the product of their mouths.

Numbers 14

4 That night all the members of the community raised their voices and wept aloud. ² All the Israelites grumbled against Moses and Aaron, and the whole assembly said to them, "If only we had died in Egypt! Or in this wilderness! ³ Why is the LORD bringing us to this land only to let us fall by the sword? Our wives and children will be taken as plunder. Wouldn't it be better for us to go back to Egypt?" ⁴ And they said to each other, "We should choose a leader and go back to Egypt."

They confess before the horrible curse to them and their future.

¹⁶ 'The LORD was not able to bring these people into the land he promised them on oath, so he slaughtered them in the wilderness.'

God is delighted when we keep up our confession; that is a sign of faith and assurance.

Hebrews 10

¹⁹ Having therefore, brethren, boldness to enter into the holiest by the blood of Jesus,

²⁰ By a new and living way, which he hath consecrated for us, through the veil, that is to say, his flesh;

²¹ And having an high priest over the house of God;

²² Let us draw near with a true heart in full assurance of faith, having our hearts sprinkled from an evil conscience, and our bodies washed with pure water.

²³ Let us hold fast the profession of our faith without wavering; (for he is faithful that promised;)

Now Faith is the substance of things hoped for, the evidence of things not seen.

But without faith it is impossible to please God: for he that comes to God must believe that He is... (Hebrew.11: 1,6)

When you open your mouth, please say what you believe and it will come to pass by the power of God.

Instead of talking unbelief it is better to be quiet and to meditate upon the power of God. If you do not open your mouth nobody else will

force you. Why curse and condemn yourself by your own words.

"Then you are trapped by your own words, and you are now in the power of someone else..." Prov.6:2

For your advantage, declare faith, dream faith, and show faith. Though you do not feel, see, touch, don't worry--it will come to pass. The longer you believe the easier it will be to transform unseen to seen. Trust God with all your heart. Jesus is the healer; there is abundant healing in faith through Jesus. You can project it into all situations. Jesus is the doer of miracles, believe it and live.

Don't be victim of the unbelief of certain religious people who deny the power of the gospel. When we quote God, power is behind him at the times. Don't be deceived.

Be always edified by the Word of God and not the words of people.

Words of people may be good but not true--that is the difference.

The Word of God may seem difficult but has life inside it.

Do not authorize your past to steal your blessings.

We both passed by many mess ups, but now we have a clear vision.

The past is over; let's continue with a real experience by faith.

Apostle Paul said that "I have not yet reached my goal, and I am not perfect. But Christ has taken a hold of me. So, I keep on running and struggling to take hold of the prize...I don't feel that I have already arrived. But I forget what is behind, and I struggle for what is ahead. I run toward the goal, so that I can win the prize of being called to heaven" (Phil.3:12-14).

Brethren, we cannot walk by feelings and experience the miracle of God neither can we know the power of the resurrection.

It is true that we are new creatures; this cannot be understood by our intellect but by the Spirit in faith.

For though we walk in flesh, we do not war after the flesh: for the weapons of our warfare are not carnal, but mighty through God...

2Cor10:2-3

It is nonsense to join people who cannot help you by the word of faith in the time of trouble.

The leader who doesn't obey the "thus saith the Lord" always leads people to self-destruction.

Moses did follow all the instructions of God without complacency to bring Israel from Egypt to the desert.

Joshua did follow the steps of Moses and success followed him.

We do not need the strange fire, the anointing fire we have in God's storage is strong enough for everybody.

Pharaoh heard the Word of God but despised it and the result was the destruction of himself and his people.

God never told Pharaoh to enter into the Red Sea—that was for Moses and Israel.

Your words can heal you or kill you, so you can be the worst enemy of your own destiny.

Even when you face a very threatening situation don't try to be whatever your body feels or perceives. Be what the Word of God says: say it, believe it, and proclaim it.

The true liberation is in your mouth, in your thoughts and strongly in your belief. As long you believe that the Lord Jesus set you free, you don't have to doubt your freedom.

That freedom cost Him His life, His freedom and His blood.

He was a prisoner that I may not be under any kind of slavery.

The faith is not a matter of pretending, imitating or seeking to impress. It is a continuing connection with the Word of God; a) in thinking b) in speaking c) in behaving d) in inner attitude e) in doing things

Nothing can avoid the control of God. He is in control and may change any difficult situation; He may create a good and better and best situation for those who grasp the truth of faith without complacence.

Therefore, I have to speak faith, to eat faith, to exchange faith, to dwell in faith.

In Christ we are new creatures; old things are passed away; behold, all things are become new (2Cor 5:17).

Many people are satisfied by ordinary when God wants them to go beyond limitations. Satan fears your future more than your past but He tries to show you the failure of the past to keep you in bondage.

God told Moses to throw down his stick. After he said to him to take it again, it was not a stick but a serpent. It turned into a miracle beyond his expectation. We also, in our new creaturehood had to throw away our philosophy, our tradition, our routine, our old way to deal with things, and grasp the spiritual realm by faith.

The Word of God is your burning bush, inside you and outside you.

You must throw your old fashioned limitations away, or you cannot reach the transformation. God Himself transformed the stick into a serpent and also the serpent into a stick. Praise The Lord.

The connection you have to Jesus is worth more than you have for humans; they are all sometimes unable to give positive assistance. They can kill you spiritually and physically because of their selfishness.

Only your faith will save your life, relying on the Word of God.

How many children of God are in trouble because of relying on somebody?

Never rely on somebody else, including your traditional partner. Sometimes trust can be replaced by distrust and all your life will go downhill.

Faith is the hand that grasps the gift of God in Jesus and makes it our own.

To dwell in integrity in the Word of God will make us different.

This is the product of obeying the Word of God and not the emotion. Emotion is not the true reality, it is another avenue the devil utilizes to seduce the children of God so be aware of it and do not be led by emotions but by the Word of God.

Even when emotion is very great, do not rush to act but rush to pray and go very deep in intercession. When you cannot stand, look for somebody who is strong in faith to agree with him in the Word rather than going to religion that will deceive you by improper compassion.

Psychology, Philosophy, Tradition, Routine never bring anointing or the presence of God at anytime.

The Word of God is one and unique for the transformation, miracle, healing, and for the anointing.

We have to close the door to these elements in our ministries and walk by faith and not by sight. We have to say faith, to dream faith, to eat faith, to digest faith and to manage everything by faith.

Do not authorize your fear to be the obstacle of the blessing. This has to be taken by faith walking in love. Many times the Lord Jesus told people before the miracle, "Fear Not," and another word, "Your Faith healed you," the third, "Sin no more."

Take the culture of Paul to forget the past and go forward for victory. Better to cover all holes in our lives which hinder the glory of God in our lives. All good fathers leave blessings to their children. We are the children of God and he promised us the blessings. God wants us to prosper, to be well. The prosperity in all things is possible through faith walking by love. When Abraham tithed to Melchizedek he was blessed: That blessing led him to get other blessings that he couldn't recover in totality. In his incarnation Jesus came and fulfills the remaining; to be the blessing to the whole world. This is the meaning of the greeting of Angels to the shepherds proclaiming that "there is good news in the earth. The good news is in the messiah who came with salvation to all humankind. Believe in Jesus and you will be saved. We have good news to share to this humanity; Jesus Christ has reconciled the people to God. The restoration includes blessings from Adam, and the fulfillment of the blessings of Abraham that came true in Jesus. The past became a history. By the shed blood of Jesus the curse was deleted; the earth purified, the heavens purified, our heart purified by the holy blood of Jesus, the second Adam.

GENESIS 14

[17] After Abram returned from defeating Kedorlaomer and the kings allied with him, the king of Sodom came out to meet him in the Valley of Shaveh (that is, the King's Valley).

[18] Then Melchizedek king of Salem brought out bread and wine. He was priest of God Most High, [19] and he blessed Abram, saying,

"Blessed be Abram by God Most High,

Creator of heaven and earth.

[20] And praise be to God Most High,

who delivered your enemies into your hand."

Then Abram gave him a tenth of everything.

GENESIS 22

[15] The angel of the LORD called to Abraham from heaven a second time [16] and said, "I swear by myself, declares the LORD, that because you have done this and have not withheld your son, your only son, [17] I will surely bless you and make your descendants as numerous as the stars in the sky and as the sand on the seashore. Your descendants will take possession of the cities of their enemies, [18] and through your offspring[b] all nations on earth will be blessed,[c] because you have obeyed me."

III
THE FALSE LOVE

Brethren it is very sad to realize that from the altar to the benches in the churches, many are hypocrites. They show love when they will get something from the other. The sacrifice can be done only for the biologic family or the close relative but for the body of Christ, they have a thousand excuses.

You cannot be free if you are cut off the branch; either you are inside or outside. It is very simple.

John 15

5 "I am the vine; you are the branches. If you remain in me and I in you, you will bear much fruit; apart from me you can do nothing. 6 If you do not remain in me, you are like a branch that is thrown away and withers; such branches are picked up, thrown into the fire and burned. 7 If you remain in me and my words remain in you, ask whatever you wish, and it will be done for you. 8 This is to my Father's glory, that you bear much fruit, showing yourselves to be my disciples.

It is clear that we cannot bear good fruit when we are outside Jesus. The LOVE that Jesus asks us is not a demand but a command.

12 My command is this: Love each other as I have loved you. 13 Greater love has no one than this: to lay down one's life for one's friends. 14 You are my friends if you do what I command.

In Galatians 6, it emphasizes that we must start with the believer.

9 Let us not become weary in doing good, for at the proper time we will reap a harvest if we do not give up. 10 Therefore, as we have opportunity, let us do good to all people, especially to those who belong to the family of believers.

Matthew 24

2 Because of the increase of wickedness, the love of most will grow cold, 13 but the one who stands firm to the end will be saved. 14 And this gospel of the kingdom will be preached in the whole world as a testimony to all nations, and then the end will come

Today many ministers are in trials because the Word of God concerning hospitality is in the trash. The consequence? They are all over the factories to help themselves.

Matthew 10

40 "Anyone who welcomes you welcomes me, and anyone who welcomes me welcomes the one who sent me. 41 Whoever welcomes a prophet as a prophet will receive a prophet's reward, and whoever welcomes a righteous person, as a righteous person will receive a righteous person's reward. 42 And if anyone gives even a cup of cold water to one of these little ones who is my disciple, truly I tell you, that person will certainly not lose their reward.

It is obvious that the wealth that the Western preachers have--if they devoted it to the gospel throughout the continents--the revival shall be everywhere in this world. Unfortunately each one wants to build his kingdom by his wealth. May God help us to have the wisdom to share what we have for the glory of God.

There are strong preachers in all the world who cannot afford the ticket to spread the gospel even in their own region. My cry is that we understand the power of unity in the body of Christ. Love is number one--not race, tribe, clan and things likewise. It is not enough, those who have plenty force the needy to give them what they have. It is time for them to bless others and not to continue saying 'God will bless you if you give to me.' You were blessed to be a blessing; do not lie to people about blessing. What you have is the blessing of God that you possess to bless others all around the world.

My friend, you have in your account 100 million American dollars and you still take from the people who cannot get even a thousand dollars together in their church, instead of giving them a life-giving project with one hundred thousand dollars. It is a simple way to chase away poverty, and get rid of your principles of selfishness. I am so sorry for this mentality. We have to change and be first the blessing to others.

Love is the fullness of the purpose of the gospel; it makes me suffer to realize how many ministers are full of lies in their promises. Children of God, we have to shine first in love before we shine in power. When somebody walks without the true love of God, the power of darkness can work inside him; this is true and does not have an alternative. Love heals and love attracts. If one of our brothers falls into sin, we have to continue to love him, to visit him, to give him whatever we can so we may communicate to him the love of God. We have to pray honestly for him and invite him to stay with us. Do not let him dwell in the hands of Satan. Anybody can sin and anybody can repent because the grace of God is still there. The love and grace of God attract us to repent. Never gossip; in love there is not the word 'gossip' but 'gospel.' We have to be very careful for the needs of our colleagues as servants of God. When they suffer we must be ready to show our love. Brethren, here it is not a matter of pretending but of demonstrating the true love of God toward the body of Christ. Pay attention to the burden of others. This can heal the wound caused by the enemy to our brethren in the Lord. If I remember the servants of a certain area of the third world who do not have the ability to buy a Bible while thousands of dollars are used for the games in holiday times in certain churches, I realize that we need the revelation from God to think about others.

Proverb: 3:3-4

³ Let love and faithfulness never leave you;
  bind them around your neck,
  write them on the tablet of your heart.
⁴ Then you will win favor and a good name
  in the sight of God and man.

²⁵ Jesus knew their thoughts and said to them, "Every kingdom divided against itself will be ruined, and every city or household divided against itself will not stand."

Matthew 5

⁴⁰ And if anyone wants to sue you and take your shirt, hand over your coat as well. ⁴¹ If anyone forces you to go one mile, go with them two miles. ⁴² Give to the one who asks you, and do not turn away from the one who wants to borrow from you.

Many times I feel very bad to realize that many Christians refuse to help others in time of need. Instead of helping one another, they are ready to gossip while Muslims are doing better at supplying the lack of their members. One day I was travelling from Tanga, Tanzania to Mombasa, Kenya. It was amazing, I met one Muslim that I didn't know paying for my bus ticket and food during that trip and he took me to my destination. It was for me a new experience and I appreciated that kindness though I didn't accept their faith. If we Christians could understand the impact of kindness and goodness, God should dwell amidst us.

When I need water or food, supply first my need instead of playing much pharisaic music. My spiritual problems cannot make you an enemy to me. God knows the truth and He will judge, not you. Give me a shelter, my brother, when I am in need and then we can talk faith, correction and others.

IV
LACK OF MIRACLE EXPECTANCY

Every day we shall expect a miracle. God is in charge and He is able to do more than enough. Believing can make God to overflow in providing for our needs and to cause any situation to turn to our favor. We serve a Miracle God. By his words we will transform the natural by the supernatural. Do not give up, your miracle is on the way, and it shall knock on your door.

Your miracle has your name on it. It cannot go to a false address; he is yours. With your eyes you shall see it; with your hands you shall touch it: do not get a limitation of double double but seven seven in Jesus' name. I already see the resurrection of two debts in my ministry. I received many financial miracles. I am expecting a special miracle of money according the multiplication of my seeds by my God. Hallelujah, I am the holy tabernacle of God and the cloud of glory is over me. How can I beg for bread when the most high walks with me? I dwell in his presence both day and night. God is good and all He does is miraculous toward the human being. The season will change in our favor. God shall bring an opportunity to bring you a sure breakthrough. By faith you shall be on the top and not beneath. Know that all things work together for our good. I feel

excited by the Word and right now I am on miracle fire traversing my entire body. God is true and his Word is a true solution in all businesses.

Expect a miracle now; get a miracle right now in Jesus' name.

Miracles prove the possibility everywhere in the name of Jesus. Possibility is everywhere for those who have the language of possibility, the heart of possibility, the brain of possibility, the vision of possibility and the dream of possibility. Let the fear, tears and doubts plaguing your faith tremble before your boldness. We were created to make a big difference by our belief.

When God told Moses that He would give Israel meat he didn't how but he believed. Because of his faith God used the wind to bring quail, which fed Israel to their satisfaction.

EXODUS 16

[11] And the LORD spake unto Moses, saying,

[12] I have heard the murmurings of the children of Israel: speak unto them, saying, At even ye shall eat flesh, and in the morning ye shall be filled with bread; and ye shall know that I am the LORD your God.

[13] And it came to pass, that at even the quails came up, and covered the camp: and in the morning the dew lay round about the host.

When Jesus told Peter about money to pay the taxes he could not imagine that He would send him to fish and find money in the mouth of a fish. He just obeyed and it came to pass.

When Jesus commanded Peter to throw the net to catch the fish, he didn't know the place but Jesus told him to throw it very near the shore and though they failed all the night, the possibility occurred by the order of the Lord Jesus.

Zekaria

[6] Then he answered and spake unto me, saying, This is the word of the LORD unto Zerubbabel, saying, Not by might, nor by power, but by my spirit, saith the LORD of hosts.

Miracles are everywhere with the word if we are in the presence of God. Anything in the hand of God always produces signs and wonders. To familiarize yourself with religious people who entertain doubt and unbelief can deceive you and kill your faith. Where the Spirit of God is, surely his manifestation shall be there.

It is not by power, nor by force, but by the Spirit of God

Roman 8

[28] And we know that in all things God works for the good of those who love him, who[i] have been called according to his purpose.

Hebrews 13
God has said,
"Never will I leave you;
never will I forsake you."[a]
⁶ So we say with confidence,
"The Lord is my helper; I will not be afraid.
What can mere mortals do to me?"[b]

My miracle is mine; if you try to steal it you will destroy your destiny.

All the time you provoke me, you are provoking the anger of God to you. I will not take revenge but He will, and He cannot forget.

I know to whom I will talk no matter what bad things you say to me, no matter how you treat me, my defender lives. The body of Christ has a great need to change, to be transformed so we can grasp the spiritual reality.

We need to change the life paradigm.

Change of mentality (to move out of carnal routine)

Change of priorities.

Change of system, focusing on heaven's benefits.

Change of conception and to see as giants.

No matter how you preach or how many people you have--your gift, your talent can bring you to a place where your character cannot keep you right. Unless you present your body as a pleasant sacrifice to God, a problem will dwell in your life. Let your body glorify the Lord. The daily fight you have is against the lust of the flesh and the lust of eyes. Our total victory depends on how we surrender our lives to satisfy the will of God and not the flesh.

Without the situation I face today I will not be what I shall be tomorrow. Praise God all the time. He knows what is next and He has a good plan for you. A plan of hope, of joy, of dignity, of elevation, of reparation, of glory, of healing and salvation.

By faith your miracle is releasing and it will knock on your door by faith. Faith is all we need in such times.

Let doubts and unbelief go far from you; you don't need them. You need a true deliverance by the Word, not by your emotions.

Believe and go free in the name of Jesus.

There is not a true deliverance if it does not come from the incorruptible Word of God.

When Lazarus died and spent four days in the tomb, Jesus came; He spoke to death to release him and it came to pass. All things are possible for those who believe. If you do not believe, you cannot see the glory of God.

To believe is the decision of the now but to refuse is your right.

Don't pretend to be what you aren't and to possess what you have not. Always submit to the Lord and resist the devil, he shall flee.

Faith chases fear, doubt, and chases all that is against the will of God. It shakes the unseen until it becomes reality.

Faith is not an imitation but is an act, a step of obedience to the Word.

In time of trouble and insecurity please do not join unbelieving or traditional religious people. They may cause your spiritual death and physical death; find a hero of faith to be your associate and partner. Join me as I follow the Word of God.

Faith is different from religious dogma; it consists of taking the Lord at His Word.

A young man called David, had faith in God and brought the people of God to the right. He refused to see his finite human nature or to be defeated because he used the name of Jehovah.

Goliath was defeated not by a carnal weapon but by the power of God moving in a young boy. Nobody could imagine the victory of David except God and himself, relying on the power of God.

We are not of them who draw back unto perdition; but of them that believe to the saving of the soul (Hebrews 10:38).

Your crisis is not for your destruction, it is for your elevation when you continue to wait joyfully for the Lord to move you up.

Don't go where others are going to look for security and care, using false and carnal strategies of Egypt. Your issue is in the hand of God. Your name is exalted in the high places where you don't think anybody knows you.

You have to know your new identity because when you receive the Lord you became a new creature. You must have a new language; the faith language—a new mentality, holy mentality, new friends--those who have the boldness to overcome the devil and to recover what he stole from you. We are here for a while. Then we shall go home very soon where the floor is made of pure gold; a country full of light and full of God's praise.

The people who do not know their identity shall be abused in time of desolation; but those who know God, they are strong and lifted up everywhere. They know that God cannot leave them nor forsake them. Praise God.

GENESIS I

[26] Then God said, "Let us make mankind in our image, in our likeness, so that they may rule over the fish in the sea and the birds in the sky, over the livestock and all the wild animals,[a] and over all the creatures that move along the ground."

[27] So God created mankind in his own image,

in the image of God he created them;

male and female he created them.

[28] God blessed them and said to them, "Be fruitful and increase in number; fill the earth and subdue it. Rule over the fish in the sea and the birds in the sky and over every living creature that moves on the ground."

In the beginning, God blessed Adam and gave him the power to multiply, to subdue the earth and to rule, being in God's abundance. When he sinned he lost the blessing and a curse replaced it. It wasn't the end of history. By Jesus Christ humanity recovered what Adam lost; and this is by faith, by renewal of the old nature when we receive Jesus as our Lord and our Savior.

V

THE FAMILIARITY OF ACTIVITIES HOSTILE TO THE ANOINTING.

Avoid sexual immorality attraction in all its kinds.

What you see, what you hear, and what you say have a big impact in your life. The place you like to visit, if it is full of jokes and ungodly subjects, you surely have found a source that will steal your anointing. The anointing is holy; it cannot dwell in an unholy affair. Alcohol and cigarettes are hindrances to your holiness. Please ask yourself the reason you wear sexy clothes; here you become an instrument that the devil will use to seduce your fellow people.

Psalm 1

[1] **Blessed is the one**

who does not walk in step with the wicked

or stand in the way that sinners take

or sit in the company of mockers,

[2] **but whose delight is in the law of the LORD,**

and who meditates on his law day and night.

³ That person is like a tree planted by streams of water,
which yields its fruit in season
and whose leaf does not wither—
whatever they do prospers.
⁴ Not so the wicked!
They are like chaff
that the wind blows away.
⁵ Therefore the wicked will not stand in the judgment,
nor sinners in the assembly of the righteous.
⁶ For the LORD watches over the way of the righteous,
but the way of the wicked leads to destruction.

God will never support adultery and immorality.

Men and women of God have the faith to build palaces and buy anything they conceive. Good, but it is not enough, they must have faith to keep themselves pure and clean before the Lord.

How can you neglect your relationship with God and you pretend to be a winner. How can you neglect your relationship with your family and claim to be right? How can you neglect the care of the ministry and claim to be a disciple of Jesus.

In the name of the Lord, let me tell you today that your faith to wear sexy clothes is a devil's lie; it is made by the devil, a snare to sin in the spirit. Be Christian inside and outside and be not subject to make an occasion of sin for anyone else.

What we see today is subject to change so it is strongly recommended to invest in the kingdom of God.

Faith, Times, Money, Vision and Plans.

Do not invest your heart in corruptible things but incorruptible.

Shake the unshakable by the power of the Holy Spirit.

Every child of God has inside him the power to transform his environment.

The strategy is not to try to change people but to be changed first.

Change is a process; it is not a magical tactic.

It is done by faith and by your decisions.

Let's walk according to the new creation.

Don't be comfortable in old things.

The time we spent in turning around the mountain is enough.

We have to press by faith to our destiny.

If you know where you are going, be sure that by perseverance you will reach your destination.

I decided to not watch sexual and fight programs on my television. I do not have time to spend with foolish things that poison my intellect, my mind and also my dream. What for? Even if many children of God like comedy, for me it is a waste of time. The more I am connected to Jesus and to His Word, the more my faith flows and the more I am contaminated in comparison to the holiness of God.

God is still in control, we have to accept the change by the transformation of our minds.

We must have faith to change our character, to heal our families and also our ministries.

No excuse of weakness. God gave us all that we need to perform what the situation requires.

If God didn't send Moses to Pharaoh, how could these Egyptians see the power of the God of Abraham?

If God didn't send Moses to the Red Sea, Israel would not see the greatness of God dividing the waters.

What can I say to the miracles of water, meat, manna, serpent, Jordan and victories over Israel's enemies?

It is terrible and full of edification.

For though we walk in flesh we do not war after the flesh, for the weapons of our welfare are not carnal, but mighty through God to the pulling down of strongholds: casting down imaginations, and every high thing that exalts itself against the knowledge of God, and bringing into captivity every thought to the obedience of Christ;

II Cor 10. 3-5

The Word of God is your burning bush, inside you and outside you.

Before you throw away your old fashioned method, you cannot reach the transformation. God Himself transformed the stick into a serpent and also the serpent into a stick. Praise the Lord.

The connection you have to Jesus is worth more than you have for humans; they are all sometimes unable to give positive results. They can kill you spiritually and physically because of their selfishness.

Only your faith will save your entire life, relying on the Word of God.

How many children of God are in several troubles because of relying on somebody?

Never rely on somebody else—including your traditional partner. Sometimes trust can be replaced by distrust and all your life will be turned downhill.

Faith is the hand that grasps the gift of God in Jesus and makes it our own.

To dwell in integrity in the Word of God will make us different.

This is the result of obeying the Word of God and not the emotions. Emotion is not the true reality. It is another way the devil utilizes to seduce the children of God so be aware of it and do not be led by emotions but by the Word of God.

Even if the emotion is great, do not rush to act but rush to pray and go very deep in intercession. When you cannot stand, look for somebody who is strong in faith to agree with him in the Word, rather than going to religion that will deceive you by improper compassion.

I put all my faith in God to have a good end. Through whatever kind of situation I may meet in my life, He is faithful.

I CORINTHIANS 15

[33] Do not be misled: "Bad company corrupts good character."[c] [34] Come back to your senses as you ought, and stop sinning; for there are some who are ignorant of God—I say this to your shame.

Psychology, Philosophy, Tradition, Routine, never bring anointing or the presence of God at any time.

The Word of God is one and is unique for the transformation, miracle, healing, and for the anointing.

We have to close the door to these elements in our ministries and walk by faith and not by sight. We have to say faith, to dream faith, to eat faith, to digest faith and to manage everything by faith.

Today, many preachers are teaching psychology and their philosophy of thinking, but that cannot replace the Word of God.

God is calling people to repent and to follow his instructions concerning dreams and destiny. If you do not have the dream of God in your life you will not reach the real destiny that is in heaven. People like to be seduced by worldly words, by worldly philosophy, by worldly speeches. Paul said that his teaching and sermons were full of God's power. God is looking for the preachers who will speak to this generation about His Son, about repentance so He may heal the land.

ROMANS 13

The Day Is Near

[11] And do this, understanding the present time: The hour has already come for you to wake up from your slumber, because our salvation is nearer now than when we first believed. [12] The night is nearly over; the day is almost here. So let us put aside the deeds of darkness and put on the armor of light. [13] Let us behave decently, as in the daytime, not in

carousing and drunkenness, not in sexual immorality and debauchery, not in dissension and jealousy. [14] Rather, clothe yourselves with the Lord Jesus Christ, and do not think about how to gratify the desires of the flesh. [c]

CAUTION! CAUTION! CAUTION!
THE MESSAGE TO ALL CHILDREN OF GOD.

CAUTION!

...Though you already know all this, I want to remind you that the Lord delivered his people out of Egypt, but later destroyed those who did not believe. And the angels who did not keep their positions of authority but abandoned their own home—these he has kept in darkness, bound with everlasting chains for judgment on the great Day. In a similar way, Sodom and Gomorrah and surrounding towns gave themselves up to sexual immorality and perversion. They serve as an example of those who suffer the punishment of eternal fire (Jude. 5-7 NIV).

CAUTION

What I want to tell you this day is: "do all that you can to escape the wrath of God to the son of rebellion." God sent his Word to all creatures, showing that without holiness no man will enter into his kingdom. Today the first thing most preachers teach is to love the world and all its contents. That is not good news, although it seems good to the flesh. People like that, dance and jump, because of prosperity, wedding, elevation but they do not care about the love of God toward others or to walk in godliness, exhibiting a behavior according the Word of God. This is acceptable by the board of the church and they think that God is with them. Not at all. God will not tolerate sin and its appearances. He is not there.

The ways Christians are behaving push many scandals in the eyes of God--no godliness and no fear of God. People are nourishing sexual immorality in the holy place and nobody rebukes this behavior. Where are we going with these pagan mentalities? Christians have to wear respectful dress that does not provoke sexual desire in the house of God. All these provoke the wrath of God and there is no way to escape His chastising.

- People become familiar with the teachings based on happiness and security based on material things and few are those who walk by faith; woe to them. God will judge all impostors and reward those who walk by faith, love and holiness. I tell you my brothers in the Lord that a teaching may be very good to hear but it still may be wrong. If it does not have a biblical foundation, it is wrong and foolish before God. Many do not preach the Word of God but philosophy and psychology. Do not follow the number of the congregation or the great name of the minister but stay in the Word of God to have the true security.

2Peter 1; 4-9

Through these he has given us his very great and precious promises, so that through them you may participate in the divine nature and escape the corruption in the world caused by evil desire.

For this very reason, make every effort to add to your faith goodness, knowledge, self control; and to self control, perseverance; and to perseverance, godliness; and to godliness, brotherly kindness; and to brotherly kindness, love. Qualities in increasing measure will keep you from being ineffective and unproductive in your knowledge of our Lord Jesus Christ.

But if anyone does not have them, he is nearsighted and blind, and has forgotten that he has been cleansed from his past sins. These verses are never taught by most modern preachers. They seem to reject the basic ingredient in salvation and feed people with emotions and all kinds of distractions. What they show are flattery, fake anointing, false revival—imagining that it can be done by noisy voices or by imitating miracles. Some miracles do not come from God, beware! The Holy Spirit gives a holy anointing to holy people. How can you pretend to have holy anointing while you refuse the Holy Spirit's instruction?

Peter said, "Be holy"

Therefore, prepare your minds for action; be self-controlled; set your hope fully on the grace to be given you when Jesus Christ is revealed. As obedient children, do not conform to the evil desires you had when you lived in ignorance. But just as he who called you is holy, so be holy in all you do; for it is written: "Be holy, because I am holy" (1Peter1: 13-15).

Do not be a fanatic or man's followers, instead, be a disciple of Jesus, knowing what genuinely pleases God. This teaching is not accepted in many Christian churches because they have their own business that is not truly devoted to the Lord. False prophecies make people comfortable because they tell them what they like to hear but not what God likes. This hour is the right time for the church to repent and return to the gospel of the cross considering the blood of Jesus and his grace greater than everything. Showing humility in the Lord, having the fear of God will bring to us good results that pride can never fulfill.

Brethren, I do not want to frustrate you but my purpose is to feed you with pure milk that will fix the mess that the devil has produced in this generation. I am 100 percent sure that God provides, He heals and He promotes but what I want to emphasize is that it is a wrong idea to put inferior things first; a true believer puts first the kingdom of God and the justice of God and all these other things will come according to the grace of God (Matt 6:33).

Loving God is necessary even when the answer to our prayers is delayed. Whether God gives me what I request or not I must love Him. He knows the reason and He knows the time. I declare that my relationship with God is not focused on material things or the good times He provides for me but it is focused on the fact that He is my God and my Savior. Nothing can be comparable to the salvation he provided for me. All that we have may depart from us but the favor of God and His grace never disappears as long we are walking in his light.

Flee dark relations. The Holy Spirit warns us to not be bound with false brothers and liars but because of carnal feelings people sympathize with them. This is very dangerous. God destroyed His own people when they joined in sexual immorality with Moabites. Balaam couldn't obtain an approval for God to destroy Israel but he knew that Israelites would curse themselves by joining the evil ceremonies of Moabite in the feast of Baal of Peor. CAUTION

While Israel was staying in Shittim, the men began to indulge in sexual immorality with Moabite women, who invited them to the sacrifices to their gods. The people ate and bowed down before these gods. So Israel joined in worshiping the Baal of Peor. And the Lord's anger burned against them (24,000 died in that plague; Num 25:1-3 9).

Do not destroy your destiny because of temporary pleasure; there is not a better and more honorable reward that a human can have than to be congratulated by God in the last day with this word "Welcome RAHA MUGISHO into the kingdom of your Father. You won, receive now your crowns for eternal life. Nothing is comparable to it. Paul made reference to it when he said, "For to me, to live is Christ and to die is gain…I desire to depart and be with Christ, which is better by far… (Phil 1:21, 23).

CAUTION!

The remaining teaching may be ordered through Godfaithful777@yahoo.com

CAUTION

These three words walk together: devil- evil – desire – sin

THE ORIGIN OF EVIL COMES FROM THE DEVIL'S SUGGESTION OR IDEA.

THE ACTION OF FULFILLING EVIL DESIRES PROVOKES SIN.

SIN ALWAYS HAS MULTIPLE NEGATIVE CONSEQUENCES.

This tells us that there is nothing good that we can gain through sin. It is a lie and a deadly distraction. If a man cleans himself from it… he will be an instrument for noble purposes, made holy, useful to the Master and prepared to do any good work.

Flee the evil desire of youth, and pursue righteousness, faith, love and peace, along with those who call on the Lord out of a pure heart. Don't have anything to do with foolish and stupid arguments, because you know they produce quarrels (2Timothy 2: 21-23).

Many people do not accept the existence of Satan; this doesn't help. Satan exists and he is the origin of evil with all its consequences. His first objective is to steal and kill and destroy. That is all He can do and never the opposite, although the picture of the fruit seems good to eat. Remember that Satan tempted our Lord Jesus but Christ did not yield to any proposal of the devil. If Satan doesn't fear to tempt our Lord, how can you pretend that he will fear you? One thing you should do is to resist him and never yield to any words out of his mouth. It is impossible for Satan to do well.

He is the liar and the father of liars, all he says is wrong and deceitful. Be aware of him and all his servants. Knowing that any person who lives in sin, whatever he does has a destructive end, so do not welcome such a person into your house, expecting to have a breakthrough.

Jesus said to the Jews who had believed him: "If you hold to my teaching, you are really my disciples. Then you will know the truth, and the truth will set you free." He replied to those who did not receive the Word: " I tell you the truth, everyone who sins is a slave to sin. Now a slave has no permanent place in the family, but a son belongs to it forever. So if the Son sets you free, you will be free indeed." Here we see that outside God, through His Son Jesus, no one else can set a man free.…. Nothing of truth rests in the mouth of the devil

Satan was a murderer from the beginning, not holding to the truth, for there is no truth in him. When he lies, he speaks his native language, for he is a liar and the father of lies. So it is very easy to discern the workers of the devil because all lie and you may expect nothing good from them at the end. If you see a so-called God's servant who lies, be sure that he is working for Satan no matter what he performs (Reference John 8: 1-47).

The devil attacked God and thought he could win but he was hurled to the earth, and his angels with him. It means that the headquarters of the devil with his angels is here on earth. He is arranging his plans for destruction and seduction using evil desire, evil works, and the goal to deviate people from the will of God. Anybody without the power of God, without protection by the blood of Jesus is nothing no matter what he may possess. He is under the influence of the demons and they can do what they want in him. He is a true slave. The demons can utilize him in many ways and they may kill him without harm to themselves.

A Christian who keeps clean his spirit and prays in faith is protected from the influence of Satan and his demons. We are called to believe in the gospel of Christ and to be warriors so we can deliver those who are under the dominion of the devil. Many marriages of saints are destroyed, not because of the wickedness of one or another, but the devil knows who between the couple is weaker and finds a door of penetration to bring ugly growing discord till the marriage is consumed. The only practice to adopt is to have compassion on your partner and pray for him so he or she recovers the knowledge destroyed by Satan. These bound persons may be preachers or have high religious titles but it doesn't disturb the devil because all that he wants to perform in them will be done without resistance. So be aware of it too, and do not neglect any precept of God. The Bible tells us to not give place to Satan. A small opening for Satan can bring a great and eternal loss.

As for you, you were dead in your transgressions and sins, in which you used to live when you followed the ways of this world and of the ruler of the kingdom of the air, the spirit who is now at work in those who are disobedient. All of us also lived among them at one time, gratifying the cravings of our sinful nature and following its desires and thoughts. Like the rest, we were by nature objects of wrath. But because of his great love for us, God who is rich in mercy, made us alive with Christ even when we were dead in transgression- it is by grace you have been saved (Eph 2:1-4).

The modernism cannot correct the Bible but the opposite is true; God never changes nor does His Word. You can interpret the Bible as your desires dictate but you will never change God. To walk according the fashion of this world is a snare to the heart and a deadly door of perversion. CAUTION We must walk by faith and not by sight or by lust; the Word of God has to lead us in all decisions. The love of this world divides people based on race, tribe, and nationality but there is no excuse to hate anybody because of his origin. The Word of God emphasizes loving everybody despite his origin. When we depart from this earth we will cease to bear our nationalities or race forever. Why create enemies for a temporary situation, which will end tomorrow? We are the children of God no matter our origin. God is one and the Father of all who believe in His Son Jesus. Do not follow the flow of people who create enmity. Repent, it is a sin which drives to murder. Resist the devil and do not lean to the spirit of vengeance; believe the Word of God. Forgive other situations that harm you. Leave the vengeance to God.

Do not let any unwholesome talk come out of your mouths, but only what is helpful for building others up according to their needs, that it may benefit those who listen. And do not grieve the Holy Spirit of God, with whom you were sealed for the day of redemption. Get rid of all bitterness, rage and anger, brawling and slander, along with every form of malice. Be kind and compassionate to one another, forgiving each other, just as in Christ God forgave you (Eph 4:29-32).

The insult and strife are not a solution, but are against the will of God; perseverance in faith and prayer can resolve many problems. Here I mean prayer in real faith, forgiving all the offence. We must have true compassion toward our offender. In that way we can have the heart to pray for them earnestly. Sometimes our own children are under the attack of Satan. They are bound and they need, not a stick, but a prayer of faith and authority to loose them. Knowing spiritual warfare is more necessary than ever; we must be sensitive to the guidance of the Holy Spirit. An unclean spirit can terrify people through a good person who is weak in the spirit. The issue is not to harm him but to deliver him by the power of the blood using the name of Jesus. But first of all we must have compassion toward others.

For though we live in the world, we do not wage war as the world does. The weapons we fight with are not the weapons of the world. On the contrary, they have divine power to demolish strongholds. We demolish arguments and every pretension that sets itself up against the knowledge of God, and we take captive every thought to make it obedient to Christ. And we will be ready to punish every act of disobedience, once your obedience is complete (2Cor 10: 3-6).

VI
THE NEGLIGENCE TOWARD GOD'S THINGS

The people of this world respect and follow principle, including principles in their organization: football, basketball, music band and the list is long but the children of God look for excuses for all God's programs. Others refuse to go to the assembly of the saints to feed their spirit. They are able to finance all outside activities by heart but when it comes to the spiritual activities they become strangers. This is another sin that makes many insensible to the Word of God.

PROVERBS 3
5 Trust in the LORD with all your heart
and lean not on your own understanding;
6 in all your ways submit to him,
and he will make your paths straight.[a]
7 Do not be wise in your own eyes;
fear the LORD and shun evil.
8 This will bring health to your body
and nourishment to your bones.
9 Honor the LORD with your wealth,
with the firstfruits of all your crops;

[10] then your barns will be filled to overflowing,
and your vats will brim over with new wine.
[11] My son, do not despise the LORD's discipline,
and do not resent his rebuke,
[12] because the LORD disciplines those he loves,
as a father the son he delights in.[b]
[13] Blessed are those who find wisdom,
those who gain understanding,
[14] for she is more profitable than silver
and yields better returns than gold.

PROVERBS 15

The heart of the righteous weighs its answers,
but the mouth of the wicked gushes evil.
[29] The LORD is far from the wicked,
but he hears the prayer of the righteous.
[30] Light in a messenger's eyes brings joy to the heart,
and good news gives health to the bones.
[31] Whoever heeds life-giving correction
will be at home among the wise.
[32] Those who disregard discipline despise themselves,
but the one who heeds correction gains understanding.
[33] Wisdom's instruction is to fear the LORD,
and humility comes before honor.

As long as you will work in accordance with the principles of God, your economy shall dwell strong and unshakable by the enemy.

Pay your tithe constantly, give your offerings and alms, and worship the Lord, read the Word of God. Walk in faith, talk faith, plant your seeds in all situations that God has authorized.

Keep your mouth from unclean words, your eyes from junky pictures, your ears from vanity, and you shall live here strong and you surely have the promise to go to the new heaven and the New Jerusalem.

That is a good end. Holiness is the nature of God, so grasp it for long term and not only in the church; it is your guarantee to enter into heaven. Your brief glory may cause your eternal shame. Take care and do not play or joke with God. He is not a joker but a fulfiller of his promises.

VII
<u>THE LACK OF TIME OF INTIMACY WITH GOD</u>

W e must know that it is a great privilege to have the almighty God who wants to meet us every day. Imagine if the president of your country gave you an appointment; this is a rare event in anyone's life. Now the owner of all the creation is at your service daily and you take it for granted. This is gross ignorance.

All these things are true because he is love and when we meet with him we return blessed and sanctified. What great favor we have to meet the Lord every day. If you are full of programs, it is wise to cancel some so you may have a time of intimacy with your Father who loves you and who wants to give you a fresh revelation. People who do not have time with God leave themselves in great emptiness. They lose the joy of the Lord and they remain Christian in name only.

Our father God is jealous. He is so disappointed when we do not have enough time to remain in his presence. As for me I never feel enough joy inside me than the times I am in the presence of God. I enjoy spending nights and days in his presence and I receive the daily revelation.

EXODUS 20

For I, the LORD your God, am a jealous God, punishing the children for the sin of the parents to the third and fourth generation of those who hate me, ⁶ but showing love to a thousand generations of those who love me and keep my commandments.

EXODUS 34

¹⁴ Do not worship any other god, for the LORD, whose name is Jealous, is a jealous God.

ISAIAH 55

Seek the LORD while he may be found;
call on him while he is near.

Psalm 100

A psalm. For giving grateful praise.
¹ Shout for joy to the LORD, all the earth.
² Worship the LORD with gladness;
come before him with joyful songs.
³ Know that the LORD is God.

It is he who made us, and we are his[a];

we are his people, the sheep of his pasture.

⁴ Enter his gates with thanksgiving

and his courts with praise;

give thanks to him and praise his name.

⁵ For the LORD is good and his love endures forever;

his faithfulness continues through all generations.

4 POINTS VERY PRECIOUS FOR THE BRIDE OF CHRIST

I – INTIMACY

The bride must have this in her daily discipline and program; to express with words the love we have to God. Here there is no shame, no tradition, no taboo but it shall be automatic from the deepest part of our hearts as we proclaim loudly the character of God, His holiness, His Power, His majesty. We manifest it with humility and strong love. No rush, no precipitation. Here is not a place to pray for requests or intercession. We minister to the Lord. This is a service loved by the Lord. God created us for such service of worship, adoration, praises. We remind God by thanking him for all He's done. God is still looking, not for just prayers but true worshippers. There is enough joy, power and anointing in this service because it involves God directly. It is strongly recommended for each believer to set this service throughout his life and to teach his children. Do not take all these blessings for granted, have the great zeal to perform them continually for your spirituality and your complete good. It will be well with your mind (Matt 22:37).

II- SERVICE FROM THE HEART

A-Giving

B-Tithes

C- Sacrifices

D- Prayers

E- Testify the love of God to others and make them part of the body of Christ

III- TO WALK WITH THE LORD IN FAITHFULNESS AND INTEGRITY

A. HOLINESS

B. LIKENESS (TO RESEMBLE GOD)
C. SPIRITUAL LANGUAGE (YES OR NO, DO NOT SWEAR OR LIE) USE AT ALL TIMES WORDS OF FAITH
D. HAVE LOVE, JOY, PEACE, PATIENCE, KINDNESS, GOODNESS, SELF-CONTROL
E. TO ACCEPT THE WILL OF GOD TO BE DONE

IV- FULNESS OF GOD'S CHARACTER

a. BAPTISM OF THE HOLY SPIRIT
b. BAPTISM OF WATER
c. HEAVENLY EXPECTATION
d. TO ASPIRE TO THE CROWNS OF GOD FOR WINNERS
e. FAITH AND BOLDNESS

CONCLUSION

I just want to remind you what the Lord told his disciples because I believe it shall help you. Although we can do much good here on earth, one thing is certain: we are still the disciples of Jesus and we cannot be greater than our master. According to the promises we received from the Lord we had to do more than Him, but because of pride and lack of love we stopped somewhere. It is unthinkable that many ministers do not consider the kingdom of God. They only follow the glory of this world and the material things they acquire by any strategy possible. That is a lie from the devil. You will see miracles and great men of power preaching a different gospel; this is called the modernism of the gospel and its source is the father of lies. Please be led by the Word of God and have a strong discernment to discover this danger. Many wonders and miracles do not come from God, pay twice the attention. The Bible tells us in Matthew 5; 17-20 "Do not think that I have come to abolish the law and the prophets; I have not come to abolish them but to fulfill them." How many ministers remember about the Ten Commandments? Most ignore them and they do not make reference to them. After Jesus finished the fasting of forty days and forty nights, the devil came to tempt him and one of the temptations was...and he showed him all the kingdoms of the world and their splendor and the devil told him: "All this I will give you, power, glory of the kingdom... he said, "if you will bow down and worship me." Jesus said to him, "Away from me, Satan! For it is written: Worship the Lord your God, and serve him only"(Lu 4: 6-7). Today the opposite is done without any effort of the devil. How many ministers are bowing down and worshipping the devil. Because of the wealth of this world, they lie, they kill, and betray themselves--shame on them. Where will you go with all these if you miss the kingdom of God? Please take time to read the warnings from Israel's history in 1Corinthians 10:1-12.

The kingdom of God is more than the wonders and fame you have on this earth. All these things have no value to God when we do not have the love of God toward the brethren and to his work. Our humility will lead us to a high and holy place. 'Seek first his kingdom of God and his righteousness, and all these things will be given to you as well' (Matthew 6: 33-34).

Be blessed
RAHA MUGISHO
THE SERVANT OF GOD

Bishop, Apôtre
MUGISHO KITUMAINI PASCAL

Printed in the United States
By Bookmasters